Collins *practical g*

PRUNING

Collins *practical gardener*

PRUNING

GRAHAM CLARKE

First published in 2005 by HarperCollins*Publishers*

77–85 Fulham Palace Road, London, W6 8JB

The Collins website address is:

www.collins.co.uk

Text by Graham Clarke; copyright © HarperCollins*Publishers*

Artworks and design © HarperCollins*Publishers*

The majority of photographs in this book were taken by
Tim Sandall. A number of other images were supplied
by David Sarton.

Cover photography by Tim Sandall

Photographic props: Coolings Nurseries, Rushmore Hill,
Knockholt, Kent, TN14 7NN, www.coolings.co.uk

Design and editorial: Focus Publishing, Sevenoaks, Kent

Project editor: Guy Croton

Editor: Vanessa Townsend

Project co-ordinator: Caroline Watson

Design & illustration: David Etherington

Editorial assistant: George Croton

For HarperCollins

Senior managing editor: Angela Newton

Design manager: Luke Griffin

Editor: Alastair Laing

Assistant editor: Lisa John

Production: Chris Gurney

A CIP catalogue record for this book is available from the
British Library

ISBN 0-00-719280-0

Colour reproduction by Colourscan

Printed and bound in Italy by L.E.G.O.

Contents

Introduction

The one thing that all gardens, whatever the shape, size or position, have in common is the ability to grow plants. Beyond this, unless you are planning to have just a lawn, with perhaps some annuals or bedding plants, you are almost certainly going to be growing a few woody plants. In their simplest form these are the trees, shrubs and wall climbers and, sometimes, woody herbaceous perennials, that are familiar to all of us. There are also fruiting plants, like apples and pears or blackberries and raspberries, and there are hedges, and roses, and vines, and even ground cover and creeping plants. All of these subjects will, at some stage in their growth, need to be pruned.

They may have outgrown their space, they may have become old or diseased, or they may have developed too much woody growth at the expense of flowers or fruits. These are the sorts of reasons why woody plants need to be pruned, and without this kind of intervention by us the plants would become ugly, misshapen or non-productive – or all of these. The purpose of this book, therefore, is to tell you how to prune the woody plants you have chosen to grow, or have inherited.

Pruning has an enormous amount of mystique about it, and it shouldn't have – it is not, as they say, 'rocket science'. Though science, in the botanical sense, does play a part, which is why on pages 26–29 we look at the anatomy of woody plants from the roots up. It is vital to know, before you cut in to a plant, both why you are doing it and whether you are doing it in the right place.

Before you proceed to design your garden, or prepare pruning schedules with

Pruning can help small flowering trees such as *Crataegus laevigata* 'Rosea Flore Pleno' produce a flush of attractive blossom during the spring and early summer

an existing garden, you should identify what type of garden you want. Are you a diligent kind of gardener – the sort that likes immaculate lawn edges, with not a weed in sight? If so, you will probably want neatly trimmed hedges, with woody plants in their proper place, flowering or fruiting to optimum potential. If this is you, then there will be much more pruning to do.

Alternatively, are you a more 'natural' or 'informal' kind of gardener, happy to allow plants to develop into their own shapes and habits? If you are more like this, you will have a much easier time of it, but probably will not have plants giving optimum performance.

The pruning of fruit plants, from the biggest apple trees to the smallest cordon gooseberries, with vines, bushes and cane fruits all demanding specialist attention, is covered in this book In detail. You should also have an understanding of how grafting (connecting a rootstock of one plant, to the top-growth of another) can influence how many plants develop, and how you should care for them.

The most important thing of all is not to be afraid. Do not neglect your pruning obligations: your plants will be much less valuable in terms of ornamentation or productiveness and they will more than likely be shorter-lived. Correct pruning can be immensely satisfying and the improvements in the plants concerned are often immediately evident, or if not a pleasant surprise a year or so down the line. So, arm yourself with the right tool – or tools – for the job, read up on the practicalities of how to do it, then get out there and be brave!

Bamboos, such as this *Phyllostachys nigra*, only require occasional thinning

Assessing Your Garden

Before you start to plant and prune, you must look at your garden dispassionately and assess which plants you are able to accommodate. Your garden is a unique piece of ground. It will have its own soil characteristic that may be entirely different to that of your neighbour's or adjoining gardens. Likewise, it will probably have a different microclimate, there may be differing natural vegetation (weeds and wildflowers) occurring and, unless it is a brand new, bare plot recently vacated by the builders, there are likely to be some ornamental or productive plants in place. These will also render the garden exclusive and distinctive. But in one important way your garden is the same as every other: it is a place to grow plants, and specifically the woody types covered by this book.

Existing features

Before you choose any new subject to plant, you should assess the area and think about what conditions you are able to provide the plants, and also where it is best to site them in your garden.

Think carefully about where to plant new subjects – an espalier-trained fruit tree will do best in a sheltered, sunny site

Take a tape measure and record the dimensions of your garden, then draw a plan on some graph paper. Show any established plants you wish to keep, as well as hard structures like paths, buildings, patios, and so on. Also, mark the positions of any fixed physical items that you will be unable to change, such as drains, telegraph poles and so on. Identify the direction the garden is facing, and the path of the sun. Slopes, ponds and eyesores such as washing lines can all be changed – some with ease, others with difficulty.

All of this information, on one sheet of paper, will give you the blueprint for your future garden.

Aspect, sun and shade

Which direction does your garden face – north, south, east or west? You can work this out by observing where the sun rises and which parts of your garden receive light at different times of day, or you can use a compass for a more accurate assessment. In the northern hemisphere, south-facing gardens are usually in sun for most of the day, whereas north-facing gardens enjoy limited amounts of sunlight; east- and west-facing gardens tend to receive more of a balance of sun and shade. As well as the aspect of your garden, you will also need to factor in features such as buildings, fences, trees and hedges, which will cast different degrees of shade.

Each orientation will impact differently on the permanent plants you grow. For example, some ivies, climbing hydrangeas and even one or two roses are perfectly suited to a house wall that gets little or no direct sunlight. But if you plant any sun-loving plant in this sort of position, you will be wasting your time and money.

Exposure to the elements

Another condition that will influence your choice of woody plants is the amount of exposure your garden has to the elements. If, for example, it is at a high altitude and/or is fully exposed to the prevailing winds, which can be bitingly cold in winter, any tall growing plants are likely to be affected adversely. You should plant the hardiest plants in such a place, and perhaps some of the lower growing types. Likewise, a sun-loving, drought-tolerant plant in a shady, boggy soil is not going to do well.

Often you can compensate for an exposed, windy garden by creating some form of shelter. At one extreme this could be a tall screen of mature poplar trees, for example, or it could be a simple slatted wooden fence just 1.2m (4ft) high.

Soil condition

You should always know the condition and type of soil you have. Is it acidic with a pH level below 7 or alkaline with pH above 7? (There are easy-to-use testing kits available from garden shops that will tell you this.)

Plants from the Rhododendron and heather family generally grow in the former, and do poorly in the latter.

Is the soil free-draining sand, or heavy, water-retaining clay? Most plants prefer the former, and whereas some, including roses, are suited to the latter, you could be creating real problems for yourself, and the plants, by getting it wrong.

There is hardly a type of soil anywhere on the planet that would not benefit from having well-rotted organic matter added. This, in the form of animal manure, or composted plant waste, should be incorporated before or at the time of planting. Organic matter can help supply nutrients to sandy soils, and help them to retain moisture; with heavy clay soils it can aid drainage and supply nutrients also.

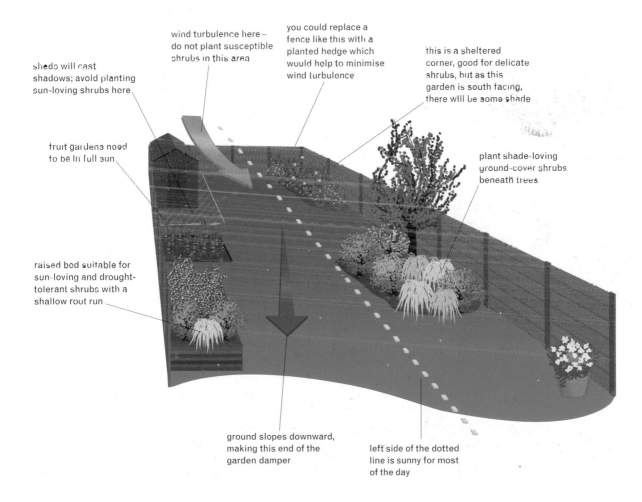

wind turbulence here – do not plant susceptible shrubs in this area

you could replace a fence like this with a planted hedge which would help to minimise wind turbulence

this is a sheltered corner, good for delicate shrubs, but as this garden is south facing, there will be some shade

sheds will cast shadows; avoid planting sun-loving shrubs here

fruit gardens need to be in full sun

plant shade-loving ground-cover shrubs beneath trees

raised bed suitable for sun-loving and drought-tolerant shrubs with a shallow root run

ground slopes downward, making this end of the garden damper

left side of the dotted line is sunny for most of the day

Reasons for Pruning

Those new to gardening frequently ask why it is necessary to prune plants at all? Surely, plants growing wild are not pruned, yet they seem to flower and fruit perfectly well! However, if one takes a closer look at those wild plants, it will be seen that this is not strictly true. The plants certainly flower and fruit, but they are usually far from what the gardener would describe as being perfect specimens. With wild plants both the quantity and the quality of the blossoms and the resulting fruits are usually far from ideal, so perhaps Nature does need a helping hand after all.

Even so, Nature does in fact have her own methods of pruning. Small branches are sometimes shed (most likely during a period of windy weather), and flowers and

Trees and shrubs left to grow wild without pruning will soon lose both their form and health

leaves die off and fall from the plants, all quite naturally. Drought, frost and even fire are all conditions responsible for removing portions of plants, usually at the growing points. Animals feed on young growths, often removing the succulent points so that trees fail to develop a single stem but instead produce many. In fact, plants are perpetually undergoing Nature's process of renewal. So, by pruning them ourselves we are actually helping to accelerate or, more correctly, control this quite normal process.

With careful and thoughtful pruning it is therefore possible to persuade a tree, shrub or climber, or even container-grown or bedding plants, to produce the flowers or fruits we desire, to grow to the size and shape we want, or to bring out the best in coloured foliage and stems. But beware, for careless and haphazard slashing with a saw or pruner can easily do more harm than good.

Keeping Plants to Size

Due to pressures of space and modern living these days, most of us are faced with smaller gardens than were enjoyed by gardeners in the past. As such, it has become essential either to select and grow plants that will achieve a modest size when fully developed, or to ensure that we limit the size of larger subjects by keeping them

Prune slowly and sympathetically; don't be tempted to lop off significant branches just for the sake of it

under control. In other words, pruning them carefully so that they do not grow too big for the space allocated to them.

In general terms, it is relatively easy to control spring-flowering shrubs by removing the longest branches, cutting at a point just above a shoot or bud low down on the plant. On the other hand, some summer-flowering kinds can be cut annually to about 8cm (3in) from the ground, and if this is carried out every year, the plants will never get the opportunity to grow larger than the length of one year's growth. A great many shrubs will tolerate cutting back to near the base of the previous year's growth, but some are liable to collapse if cut back harder.

Hedge trimming

Perhaps the most common example of pruning to keep plants to size is the case of trimming hedges. A hedge is, after all, usually a series of shrubs growing in a line. When these need trimming it is to stop them from outgrowing the space allocated to them. To grow and keep a neat, formal hedge requires more than simple trimming once or twice a year: there is a specific form of training that is often required, and the timing of the trimming can also be crucial. (See Hedges, pages 52–57 or specific plants by name in the Directory section, pages 58–92.)

Pollarding

Another, much more drastic, technique for reducing the size of a tree's crown is the practice of pollarding, which is most often seen in street trees in urban areas. Generally, a trunk with a few main branches is allowed to develop, but all other top growth is cut away. It is a very effective way to control large trees in tight spaces (see page 35).

Effective pruning is about keeping a plant in good shape and confined to the space it was intended to fill

Maintaining Shape & Habit

Most trees and shrubs look their best when they are allowed to grow naturally, and in a naturalistic setting it is always advisable, wherever possible, to encourage and retain a plant's normal shape. Trained plants, or those trimmed to a formal shape, are exceptions to this rule.

However, even in a natural and informal setting vigorous, awkwardly placed shoots can spoil the appearance of a plant, and if one part of a plant becomes more vigorous than another this can cause the overall look to become unbalanced.

Shrubs that have grown out of balance can be reshaped if these guidelines are followed:

1 – Remove straggling branches to a shoot or bud within the main bulk of the plant.
2 – Carefully but systematically reduce the number of growths on the 'good' side of the plant.
3 – Cut back weak shoots hard, and strong shoots lightly on the 'bad' side of the plant.
4 – Feed the plant with a good general fertilizer.
5 – Mulch with compost or manure.

When stems grow across one another at awkward angles they can rub together, creating wounds and leading to increased risk of disease

TIP

It is not only shrubs that require pruning to improve flowering. Many of our summer bedding and border plants need attention, perhaps better described as 'pinching back' or 'deadheading' rather than pruning (see pages 42 and 44).

Remember the general pruning principle that the strong shoots should be lightly pruned, while the weaker shoots need hard pruning. The reason for this is that hard pruning stimulates vigorous growth, so cutting back strong growths will merely encourage more vigorous shoots to be produced which will accentuate the unbalanced shape further. Similarly, hard pruning will stimulate the weaker shoots into putting on considerably more growth.

Removing Unhealthy Growth

Plants that are not maintained – that is, pruned regularly or at least annually – can often become a dense mass of tangled branches. This means that the shoots in the middle of the mass are deprived of light and air, and are prone to dying back. During windy weather the stems can rub together, causing injury to themselves and the branches they are rubbing against. All of these conditions lead to a greatly increased risk of disease.

It is frequently necessary therefore to 'open out' certain plants to enable sunshine and air to reach every branch and shoot, so ripening the wood and swelling the buds. It is always advisable to remove unhealthy growth, as well as those shoots that are straggly and misshapen. Without the removal of weak and feeble shoots, the wood will not be productive of flowers and fruits. Its removal will also facilitate ripening of the remaining wood. Dead and diseased wood should also be cut away back to clean, healthy wood. Burn these diseased prunings before the problems have time to spread to susceptible neighbours.

Pruning out pests and diseases

The following are gardening troubles that can be wholly or partly treated by pruning.

Aphids – sap-sucking blackfly, greenfly, etc.
Treatment: pinch out affected shoots or leaves.

Brown rot – fungal disease affecting mainly apples and pears, which appears as a brown spot that spreads to affect the whole fruit.
Treatment: remove all mummified or rotten fruits remaining on the tree after harvesting.

Canker – bacteria that affects mainly apples and pears, a tell-tale sign is gum oozing from a cut or wound.
Treatment: prune out infected wood.

Caterpillars – a particular problem when they bore into stems.
Treatment: cut out infected branches.

Coral spot – disease of dead wood on various trees and shrubs, easily identifiable by pink pustule-like fungus.
Treatment: remove to healthy wood.

Fire blight – bacterial disease of trees and shrubs from the rose family which appears as brown patches on leaves leading to rot.
Treatment: remove to healthy wood.

Leaf miners – insect pests that burrow under the leaf layers of various plants.
Treatment: pick off affected leaves.

Powdery mildew – disease found on various plants visible as a white, powdery covering.
Treatment: pinch out or cut away affected growth.

Silver leaf – fungal disease of certain fruit trees, including cherry trees, almond trees, etc, in the form of a brown discolouration of the wood and, often, a silvery sheen to leaves.
Treatment: cut out infected wood before mid-summer.

Woolly aphid – insect pest found on various fruit trees, which covers itself with a fluffy, white waxy coating.
Treatment: cut out badly infected wood.

Aphids are fast-breeding, sap-sucking insects which should be dealt with as soon as they are noticed

Canker bacteria is a nasty condition that affects fruit trees

Coral spot is easily identified by its distinctive pink, pustule-like fungus

Woolly aphid afflicts fruit trees and should be quickly checked

Improving Flowering

Decoration is what gardening is all about, and we would be failing, as gardeners, were we to allow trees, shrubs and other plants, to produce less than their optimum decorative effect.

Usually, the smaller a plant becomes, the more flowers it produces. Pruning therefore reduces the amount of wood, and so diverts energy into the production of larger, though fewer, flowers. It is interesting to observe an unpruned butterfly bush (*Buddleja davidii*) with its flower spikes some 10cm (4in) in length. Prune the plant correctly, and the following summer the blooms could even be 30cm (12in) in length – three times as long.

However, before we can prune a plant to improve its flowering ability, we must understand its characteristics, as this will govern the technique needed, and the correct timing. We must know whether the plant blooms on the current year's growth,

Regular pinching out or deadheading of dead or dying blooms will improve a plant's health

Deadheading improves flowering performance and the general renewal of a plant with blooms

Other forms of pruning

Some jobs carried out in a garden are forms of pruning, although they are hardly recognized as such.

Cutting the lawn: Trimming grass is a kind of pruning, in that one is reducing the size of individual grass plants.

Cutting flowers: cut a sprig of flowers for home decoration, particularly from a woody plant, and you are simply pruning the plant whilst it is in flower. You should endeavour to follow the rules of pruning, by using a sharp cutting tool, and to cut above a bud, preferably one that is facing out from the centre of the plant.

Cutting back perennials: At the end of the growing year a perennial border should be tidied up. Old, dying topgrowth should be cut back to ground level (unless seedheads are required for winter decoration). Perennials treated in this fashion are being 'pruned'.

Tree surgery: This is an extreme form of pruning, usually done to maintain a mature tree in a healthy condition. Working high up in a tree with powered saws is a frequent requirement, so it is a sensible option to employ the services of a professional tree surgeon.

or whether it produces flowers from shoots that are one or more years old. It would be disastrous to prune, during spring, a shrub from the latter group, such as lilac (forms of Syringa) or the mop-head hydrangeas, as all the one-year-old shoots stocked with flower buds would be removed. The pruning of these plants is carried out as soon as possible after the flowers have faded.

The summer and early autumn flowering shrubs, such as tree mallows (Lavatera) and St John's wort (Hypericum), flower at the end of the current season's growths. To give the flowering wood the maximum time to develop, these shrubs are pruned in early spring, as growth starts.

As ever, there are always certain plants that defy the rules: for example, *Jasminum nudiflorum* (winter jasmine) does not fit neatly into any pruning category. It may be enough to cut out old and redundant growths, yet a good display of blooms is obtained when many of the shoots that have flowered are cut back to within an inch or so of the old wood as soon as the last blooms fade in spring.

Improving Fruiting

It generally follows that flowers ultimately lead to fruit. Therefore, if you want to maximize a plant's potential for fruiting, more or less the same pruning guidelines as for flowering plants apply: to continually aim to encourage productive growth. Each type of fruiting plant, however, requires a different method of pruning, which is why we have devoted a large section to them later in this book. Always ensure that you follow the correct procedure for the fruit trees in your garden.

Thinning out

Farmers and gardeners alike always desire the largest possible crops, but where fruit is concerned there can come a time when the plant bears too many fruits, all of which are small. If the crop is thinned out well before ripening – another form of pruning – the remaining fruits will develop into appreciably larger specimens.

Soft fruit

The world of soft fruit can be particularly daunting to the newcomer. For example, with black currants fruit is produced on one-year-old shoots, and a 'renewal' system of pruning is required. With red currants, however, the fruit is borne on short spurs from a permanent framework of old wood. Don't worry. Once the simple techniques have been grasped, luscious crops will soon be the result.

A well-pruned fruit tree will consistently reward you with abundant crops, such as this 'Fiesta' variety of apple

This Mahonia has been regularly cut back, resulting in vibrant, colourful foliage

Improving Foliage & Stems

The rule of thumb here is that leaves are produced only on current season's growth. The more vigorous this growth, the larger and more profuse will be the foliage. Also, in plants with coloured leaves the hues will be more vivid and intense. For this reason, many vigorous shrubs grown for their foliage are pruned hard annually.

Some deciduous shrubs, such as *Cornus alba* (dogwood) and *Salix alba vitellina* (willow), have coloured barks and are grown

The stunning bark of *Cornus alba* 'Sibirica' is best on young stems, so prune hard back in early spring to achieve the finest colour

This Elaeagnus shrub is badly in need of attention, with straggly stems growing in every direction

purposely to enhance the winter garden. The most effective colour is produced on young stems, so these shrubs should be cut as close to the ground as possible in early spring.

Pollarding (see page 11) is carried out to keep the heads of certain trees within bounds, but its principle can also be applied to create shrub-like effects with trees such as Eucalyptus. Hard annual pruning will cause the plant to produce masses of stems, each carrying many of the blue-grey rounded or 'juvenile' foliage highly sought after by flower arrangers and gardeners alike.

Tools & Equipment

As with most practical jobs, the key to success is not only knowledge of what you are doing, but having the right tool for the job as well. The equipment needed for pruning varies hugely, from small, lightweight secateurs, through to the large, heavy-duty loppers and powered saws used by the professionals.

As one's interest in gardening develops, which usually accompanies the acquisition of progressively larger gardens, so more and more pruning tools will become useful. For example, even the newest, most inexperienced gardener would be well advised to invest in a good pair of

secateurs. They are versatile, easy to use, and do not cost a fortune. The more experienced gardener will perhaps grow some fruit trees, where loppers, long-handled pruners and ladders may be necessary. Trimming hedges, pruning thick branches from mature trees, cutting flowers: all these jobs require different tools in order to be properly effected.

Saws

A pruning saw is needed for removing those branches that secateurs or loppers cannot cut; as a general guide anything over 2.5cm (1in) in diameter should be tackled with a saw. There are many different kinds of pruning saw. The larger ones can be used for felling and cutting up trees, as well as removing large tree limbs. Smaller saws should be used on small trees and shrubs that need to have their growth thinned.

Curved pruning saw This is also known as a Grecian saw, and is one of the best. It has a slightly rounded handle and blade, tapering to a narrow point at the end of the blade. It bites readily into the wood on the backward stroke, and when sharp cuts quickly and cleanly. Some models are

There is a wide range of pruning tools available for many different jobs; accumulate them as necessary

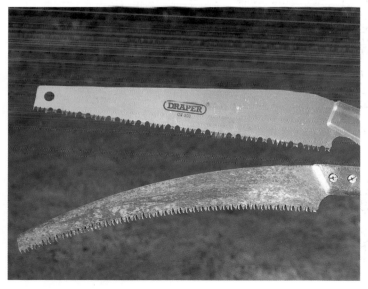

Grecian saws are ideal for slicing through inaccessible branches

Any old saw?

Only saws specifically designed for use in the garden should be employed for pruning jobs. A carpenter's saw, for example, is not suitable for cutting 'green' living wood, because the teeth get clogged with the soft, moist sawdust, making the saw bind. Also, this kind of saw is likely to be too large to fit in some of the small gaps between tree branches. Pruning saws have wide-set teeth, to make the cut a little wider than the thickness of the blade, so there is less risk of jamming.

Always use a saw that has been designed for the job in hand. This bow saw will tackle all well spaced branches

designed to fold, with the blade closing into the handle for easy storage; the added bonus to these is that they can be carried around with you in a pocket or pouch.

Bow saw This has a curved steel tube frame with a straight, detachable saw blade that is held taut between the arms of the frame. It is released by a small device, usually a twist nut or short handle, at one end. There is a row of sharp teeth set on the outside of the blade, enabling the saw to cut on both the forward and return strokes. Bow saws are capable of tackling all branches, as long as there is enough space to move. Replacement blades are available.

Pruning saw A general-purpose pruning saw is similar to a carpenter's saw, but is better adapted to cutting 'green' wood. It is good for cutting wood where access is difficult for a bow saw. It will often have small teeth at the tip of the blade to help start you off, and then the larger teeth, closer to the handle, assist faster cutting.

Alternatively, there are two-edged pruning saws, which have larger teeth on one side than the other. The initial cut can be made with the finer toothed edge, to be finished off with the coarser teeth. This type of saw, however, is unsuitable for dealing with branches growing close together, as the unused cutting edge may cause grazing damage to nearby growth.

Safety is the main point to bear in mind with saws, as it is easier to cut yourself with the exposed, open blade of a saw than it is with the closed blades of secateurs or shears. The latter, scissor-action tools are usually used in a more precise and considered way.

This folding pruning saw has the built-in safety feature of a retractable blade

Secateurs

A pair of secateurs is probably the most important pruning tool. Once you find a pair that suits you, you will use them for years. Using secateurs requires no special skill, and relatively little effort.

Of all the secateurs on the market, there are really only two main types of cutting action: anvil secateurs with one cutting blade, and bypass secateurs, with two. The latter types are also sometimes called parrot-beak secateurs, derived from the blade shapes of some models.

Anvil secateurs These have a soft metal anvil that supports the plant stem while the single hard-metal blade cuts through it. Do not twist the secateurs when cutting as this strains them and, in time, the blade will cut off-centre. Also, keep the blade sharp to avoid its tendency to squash the stems.

A basic set of anvil secateurs, designed for straightforward cuts around the garden

Bypass secateurs These cut like a pair of scissors, though only one of the blades has a cutting edge. Some secateurs are designed to reduce the aches and pains caused by excessive pruning, by having a swivelling lower handle. Similar, but less commonly seen, are 'manaresi' secateurs, often used for pruning vines. These tools have two blades, both with straight cutting edges that meet as the cutting action is completed.

Ratchet secateurs Usually anvil secateurs, these have a special mechanism (the ratchet) that makes it possible to cut through a hard or thick stem in stages. When you squeeze the handle, the blade cuts into the stem. You can then release the pressure on the handle and the blade stays where it is, until you squeeze again. This is good for gardeners with smaller hands, or for those who tire easily.

A range of bypass secateurs. The shapes of the grips are generally designed for ease of handling, particularly over long periods of time

When to use secateurs

DO use secateurs for:
- pruning woody stems of finger-thickness or less
- cutting back perennials
- deadheading
- cutting flowers for indoor display
- preparing cuttings for propagation

Do NOT use them for:
- cutting wood thicker than a finger (which will put strain on the blades, perhaps causing them to become offset)
- ripping into plastic bags of fertilizer or compost (as this may cause fragments of plastic to jam in the mechanism)
- cutting wire or other metals (which will damage the blades)

Long-handled loppers are designed for reaching up and into the heart of a tree or shrub

Choosing a model

Most types of secateurs are made of carbon steel, and the blades of some of the more expensive models are coated with a non-stick material which prevents sap from fouling them, and makes cutting easier. The handles, or more correctly handgrips, can be made of either moulded nylon or fibreglass, or light aluminium alloy coated in moulded vinyl. Models differ in both size and shape, and it is important to handle them thoroughly in the shop, to assess the comfort and 'feel' before you make your purchase. Also, check to see that there is a 'shock absorber' between the handles; this avoids pinching and injuring your fingers.

Using secateurs

Position the stem to be cut close to the base of the blade where it can be held firmly. If the cut is made with the tip, the blades are liable to be strained or forced apart. Always make a clean, straight cut, and never be tempted to twist either your wrist, or the secateurs. If you cannot cut through a stem cleanly, it is likely that the stem is too big, so you should use loppers or a saw instead.

Good maintenance is important, and before putting the secateurs away it is sensible to put a spot of oil on the pivot and spring to keep them in good condition.

Loppers or long-handled secateurs

Still on the theme of secateurs, finally we come to these modified versions of the parrot beak or anvil type. Fixed handles can be some 45cm (18in) in length, and with telescopic models this can almost be doubled. These tools are useful for cutting out old, hard wood that is too thick and tough for ordinary secateurs. The blade or blades open wide, and with the longer handles extra leverage and a greater reach than usual is available.

Whereas the operator can use a normal pair of secateurs with one hand, both hands are required for these long pruners. Make sure that the loppers you buy have the all-important shock-absorbing stoppers set just beneath the cutting mechanism, as this will make cutting much easier on your joints.

Safety with secateurs

There are a number of safety points to watch for with secateurs, both when they are in use, and out of season when they are stored away.

- Keep the blades closed and ensure that the safety catch is always on when they are not being used.
- Never force the secateurs to cut wood that is too thick for them: they are usually capable of cutting stems up to finger thickness.
- Immediately you have finished using them, clean the sides of the blades with emery paper (to remove caked-on plant debris and drying sap, which could spread certain plant viruses), and follow this by a wipe over with an oily cloth.
- Store the secateurs in a high, dry place, such as a shelf, well out of the reach of children.

Tree Loppers or Long-arm Pruners

If you do not enjoy ladders or heights, then you would be wise to invest in a tree lopper or tree pruner – they are invaluable for removing high branches which would otherwise be well out of reach. Basically they are bypass-type secateurs attached to the end of a pole, which may be extended to between 2–3m (6–10ft) in length, according to your requirements. This will effectively give you access to stems some 4.5m (14ft) from the ground.

The cutting blade is put into action by a cord or wire attached to a lever at the bottom end. As an optional extra some

Tools & Equipment

Tree loppers – basically secateurs on a pole – take the strain out of cutting back high and inaccessible branches

> **TIP**
> Some models of tree loppers are available with a pruning saw or fruit picking attachment (the latter is essentially a basket which fits close to the blade for picking fruit without the need to climb). Remember that this tool also requires the use of both hands, one to hold and one to operate,

models offer a lightweight pre-tensioning reel for easier control of the cord.

The cutting mechanism is typically designed to cut stems up to 3cm (1.5in) thick. Some models also offer an adjustable head assembly, enabling the lopping heads to rotate through an angle of 180°, so that the operator can adjust to the angle needed for a clean cut.

Pruning Knives

All-purpose garden knives are suitable for cutting string, opening bags of compost, generally gouging, probing and cutting things without much finesse. A pruning knife, however, should be considered an altogether different kind of instrument. To start with it must be sharp; it is much more dangerous in a blunt state and is next to useless for cutting. Oilstones or carborundum stones are required to keep knives sharp.

Pruning knives are heavier than other garden knives, they are bulky too, and often have a slightly curved handle with a concave blade. The curve of the blade helps you apply

The curved blades of some pruning knives enable the user to apply more pressure in the cut

Hand shears are useful for cutting the shoots and slender stems of hedges – often several at a time – but they will not cope with more heavy-duty pruning

Gloves

Most gardeners set aside a pair of old gloves for use outdoors, but never is it more important to have a stout pair than when you are faced with a bed of roses to prune. A pair of well-stitched leather gloves will protect your hands against minor cuts and grazes. Woollen or thin cotton gloves are of no real use at all here. Ideally, choose leather gauntlet gloves to keep out thorns. Cowhide and pigskin leather are the toughest forms, perfect for pruning prickly plants. Goat, sheep and deer skin options are often more comfortable, but are much less durable.

When choosing leather gloves, flex your hands and fingers to assess the fit and comfort. They should feel smooth inside; if not, look for a better pair – it is worth spending a little extra.

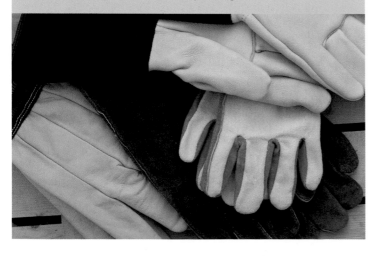

pressure when attempting to sever thicker stems. Some of the more expensive options also have a small pruning saw that folds into the handle.

Using a pruning knife

When pruning, hold the branch that is to be cut below the point where the knife comes into contact. With the knife behind the branch, just below the level of the chosen bud, make the cut by drawing the knife upwards, at an angle, to finish just above the bud. A pruning knife should be kept just for this purpose, and not used for cutting other things.

However, apart from the severing of whole branches, pruning knives do have other legitimate uses: gouging or grubbing out rotting material from wood, prior to the area being painted with a wound sealant, and paring smooth the bark after sawing off large branches.

Hand Shears

As you will see later, clipping hedges is very much an act of pruning, and by far the best tool for this is a pair of hand shears. Clipping hedges is not the only use hand shears can be put to: heathers, lavender and other clump-forming shrubs benefit from a yearly once-over with a pair of shears to remove the dead flowerheads, as well as straggly or vigorous shoots.

Most shears have straight, carbon steel blades with a 'notch' set at the base of the blade for cutting thicker stems. The blade lengths come in various sizes, most often 15–25cm (6–10in). There should be shock absorbers to prevent jarring to your wrists, and an adjustable tension nut to return the blades to their optimum cutting position. When buying a pair of shears 'test' the weight and size of the tool before you part with your money.

Telescopic handled shears are available for reaching up to taller hedges. Single-handed shears are available, too. These will only cut small, soft growths, and are perfect for long grass growing next to a wall where a lawnmower cannot reach.

Powered Hedge Trimmers

These are a quick mechanical means of cutting a hedge, and are ideal for gardeners with large expanses of vigorous hedging. Hedge trimmers have two blades, one on top of the other, each with teeth so that as one blade is drawn backwards and forwards, the stems to be cut are trapped between the teeth.

Hedge trimmers may be powered by mains electricity or petrol, with some forms operating on rechargeable batteries. The total weight of the trimmer, which is affected by the length of the cutting blade, is dependent on the type of power required. For example, a battery-operated version is most likely to be the lightest in weight, as a greater amount of energy would be required to power a heavy machine. Conversely, petrol-driven motors can be extremely powerful, and are better suited to powering heavier models. If a power point is within a reasonable distance from the hedge, this is often the best option for the average gardener who does not need to use the trimmer more than a couple of times in the year.

Chain Saws

Chain saws are used for felling trees and cutting larger logs. They certainly make light work of all heavy wood, but can be dangerous if not used sensibly. This is why you should only consider them if you have received formal training in their use. Better still, allow a professional to undertake any work that requires this tool to be used.

If you are intent on using one yourself, hiring may be the best option for you as they are expensive items of equipment. They run on petrol, and extreme care should be taken when operating them, particularly when refuelling. A particular danger is if you hit a knot in the wood you are cutting, as this can cause the chain 'bar' to kick out and momentarily you will have lost control of a

powerful, heavy, fast-moving and lethally sharp piece of equipment.

Hedge trimmers make short work of cutting back large expanses of shrub

Safety Gear

Eye protection is extremely important when pruning, particularly if you are using power equipment. With a chain saw you would be best advised to wear a hard hat with attached visor. For hedge trimmers and hand tools, plastic goggles are usually sufficient.

Protecting your ears is only necessary when using power equipment, and certainly if you use it on a regular basis you would be foolish not to use some form of protection. Whereas earplugs are generally sufficient for protection against the noise of lawn mowers and other general garden power tools, chain saws are relatively noisy, so proper ear defenders, which completely cover the ear, are necessary.

It is a sensible idea to wear eye protection during all forms of pruning and ear defenders whenever you use noisy power tools

Ladders & Supports

A rigid, sturdy ladder is necessary when pruning high branches. Trees over 2m (6ft) in height are difficult to get at, unless you have a pair of long loppers, but even these may be difficult to use effectively.

A great many households possess an aluminium alloy ladder. These are generally better than wood; certainly lighter, and without the risk of attracting woodworm, dry rot and other forms of wear and tear that can take their toll on wood. Ladders that are in less than perfect condition should not be used for pruning, as the tree or object against which they are laid will very often not be solid enough to bear enormous amounts of weight. One little slip and the rotten ladder may crumble beneath you.

It is worth investing in a decent aluminium ladder if you have lots of high pruning to do

Scaffolding

Ask any builder if they prefer working high on a ladder or on secure scaffolding, and they will all choose the latter. Where pruning is concerned scaffolding only becomes relevant when working on long, high hedges or wide trees where there is a large amount of surgery required.

Scaffolding does not always have to be the sort of bolted iron tubes found erected against buildings. There are several forms of kit scaffolding available for smaller building maintenance tasks – and other jobs, like pruning. This is, perhaps, another item of equipment that is better hired when needed, rather than purchased outright.

In addition to the scaffolding itself, you will almost certainly require boards on which to stand. These should be placed carefully and secured to the scaffold.

Ladder safety

Examine any ladder before using it, paying particular attention to rungs, treads and crossbars. When using a metal ladder, take extra care to avoid overhead cables. For added safety it would be a good idea to invest in a type with serrated flat-topped rungs, and rubber serrated feet and end plugs. Extension ladders give even greater height, but stepladders provide better stability.

Rope supports

Wherever possible secure the ladder or scaffold to the tree you are working on by tying it with rope or strong garden line; string would simply not be strong enough in case of a mishap. Jute, flax and polyethylene lines are also available.

Where very large and heavy branches have to be pruned, it is important that rope is used to support and lower them, to avoid damage to the tree and its surroundings.

Clean all pruning tools after use to prevent rust and malfunction – it is well worth the effort!

Maintenance & Cleaning

Shears and secateurs are two hand tools that will benefit from attention paid to them. First and foremost, it is essential to scrape or peel off the ingrained mud or dirt which cakes itself on to the tool during use. The metal parts should be wiped over with a wet rag, and then dried. Rust will soon get a hold if the metal is not dried at this stage.

To prevent rust, simply wipe the blade with an oily rag, and keep working parts well lubricated. It is not necessary to soak the tool in heavy oil, such as motor oil: a three-in-one mixture is ideal.

It is not only the metal parts of pruning tools that need attention. Wooden handles benefit from a wipe over with linseed oil. This will soak into the wood, giving it an in-depth protection, preventing cracking due to dryness.

Sharpening blades

The one thing all pruning tools have in common is that they 'cut'. This may seem obvious, but essentially they can only do the job required of them if they are sharp. What is less obvious is that the more blunt a blade is, the more dangerous it is; it is more likely to slip across wood whilst under pressure, and the damage a blunt blade can cause to the body can be far greater than that caused by a sharp blade.

Sharpening blades does not take long, and it makes the tool both easier and safer to use. Fine emery paper can be used to remove the initial grime on secateurs, as well as to hone the blades. Alternatively, a small oilstone can be used for sharpening. Oil or carborundum stones need careful handling; they are brittle and likely to break if dropped. The stone is lightly oiled, and the knife or secateur blade edge is rubbed along it at a fairly acute angle. If you see the original edge, follow it.

Wound sealants – a good idea?

Up until just a few years ago, it was recommended that all large cuts, say over 2.5cm (1in) in diameter, should be covered with a wound sealant. This, it was thought, would protect the heartwood until a callus could grow over the exposed surface and so seal it. Today, however, it is known that these sealants do not assist the wood's healing process, and may actually hinder it. No paint has so far proved totally impermeable to water and air, the two main carriers of plant diseases. Even commercial fruit growers, whose livelihoods depend on the health of their trees, are now reluctant to use such sealants.

Broken or improperly cut branches heal very slowly, if at all, and because of the large surface area of exposed wood, can make the perfect entry point for insect pests, fungal diseases and virus infection. The important point to remember, now that sealants are not recommended, is that any rough edges to the cuts should be made smooth with a pruning knife, without actually enlarging the wound.

Understanding Plants

Although it is not our intention to make this book a serious study on the theory of botany, a basic understanding of the ways plants work can usually dispel a considerable number of pruning myths. Like a good surgeon, the gardener who understands the anatomy of his patients invariably does the best work.

We have already seen why it is important to prune plants, but when taking a pair of secateurs to a branch it is equally important to know exactly where the cut should be made. To know where, you will need first to understand how plants extend themselves, and you will need to be able to identify different types of buds.

Basic Anatomy

It is important to understand the make-up and anatomy of the plant you are dealing with before you can prune it effectively

The principal organs of all plants are relatively few. There are the flowers, the leaves, the buds (which are future leaves or stems in embryo), the stems and the roots. All of these are linked together by the vascular system, which moves water and

What is photosynthesis?

This is the chemical process that takes place in all of the green parts of a plant; the plant takes in molecules of carbon dioxide from the air, and water through the roots, which are 'excited' by the light and warmth of the sun. When this is all combined with the presence of chlorophyll, glucose is produced. The plant uses this sugar to increase its biomass or, in other words, grow.

minerals up from the roots to the leaves. Any water that remains after transpiration – evaporation via pores in the leaves – is then redistributed throughout the plant.

Extension growth is generally made just below the topmost (apical or terminal) bud. This bud imposes a phenomenon that botanists these days refer to as 'apical dominance'. In other words, the plant's hormones inhibit the growth of the buds on the sideshoots or 'lateral' stems (see How Plants Grow, below).

How Plants Grow

Hormones (auxins, gibberellins and kinins) control the growth rates of plants. Auxins were discovered first, and named from the Greek *auxe*, meaning 'increase'. They are produced in the growing tips of plants, and distributed from there via the sap back through the stems to the roots. For this reason we know that there are two separate sap-flows in plants: one up and one down. The greatest concentration of auxins is always highest near the growth points, in the region where the plant's cells are dividing and active growth is taking place.

There are different optimum auxin levels for each part of a plant, increasing as it gets closer to the growing tips. The roots need least of all, the buds a little more, the lateral

shoots more still, and the main stems need most. If the normal hormone balance of a plant is disrupted through, say, the pruning of a leader – the main growth point and source of auxins – the auxin level in the whole plant is lowered.

Lateral stems will find the new level to their liking and react by producing growth; similarly some buds will probably open. This is why 'pinching off' of stem tips will stimulate branches into growth lower down on plants, encouraging the plants to become bushier. Eventually the newly stimulated growth points will themselves produce sufficient auxins to establish their dominance over the rest of the plant.

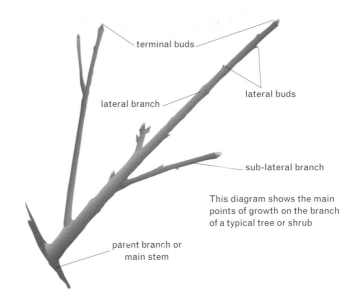

terminal buds

lateral buds

lateral branch

sub-lateral branch

This diagram shows the main points of growth on the branch of a typical tree or shrub

parent branch or main stem

Buds are the most obvious early indicators of a plant's growth, heralding new flowers, stems and leaves

Buds and branches

Buds are embryonic shoots of plants, containing the beginnings of flowers, stems and leaves.

Apical or terminal bud This is located at the very tip of a stem and controls its ultimate length. If the terminal bud is injured or removed in the act of pruning, adjacent buds will sprout into growth. In some plants there is a naturally high level of auxins,

making 'apical dominance' obvious. Christmas trees, for example, are spire-like for this reason; so much auxin is made in the vicinity of the leader that all the other branches are mere side shoots in comparison.

Lateral bud Most of these buds develop into leaves and shoots in their first growing season. They are usually formed at the 'node' where a leaf joins a stem.

Dormant bud This is a lateral bud that for one reason or another, has decided to stay inactive for perhaps a number of years. Pruning nearby is likely to stimulate growth.

Vegetative bud Many young buds are thin and green and capable of producing only leaves rather than flowers or fruits. These are known as vegetative buds. Stimulus can induce them to become larger, fatter flower buds, so we prune to encourage them on flowering shrubs and fruit trees and bushes.

Adventitious bud These do not actually come into existence unless there is a major injury to the shoot and there are no dormant buds nearby to take over. Adventitious buds are only formed by trees and shrubs when and where they are needed.

Framework

Trees and shrubs vary enormously in the size and shape of their above-ground growths. A stem or trunk may be long, short, thick or thin, depending on the species and the way it has been trained. The reason why a woody plant develops a branched habit is to expose the maximum leaf area to the sun, and therefore optimize 'photosynthesis'. Water and nutrients are transported from the roots to the leaves through the trunk of the tree. Conversely, foods taken in or manufactured by the leaves are returned through the trunk to build new root tissue, or stored as food.

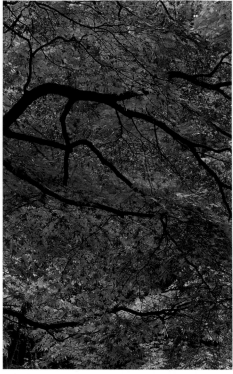

Healthy leaf growth depends upon maximum exposure to sunlight in order to facilitate photosynthesis

Suckers and water shoots

There are two types of growth that exasperate the gardener: suckers and water shoots. Suckers are leafy stems arising at the crown of the tree, or from the roots. Their connections with the roots are so good, they often grow faster than the original plants, hence the desirability of removing them before they take over.

Water shoots are strong growing vegetative shoots arising from, for example, an adventitious bud on the trunk. The shoots will, in time and if treated properly, flower and fruit in the normal way. They are usually numerous and crowd one another, so thinning out or complete elimination is to be recommended.

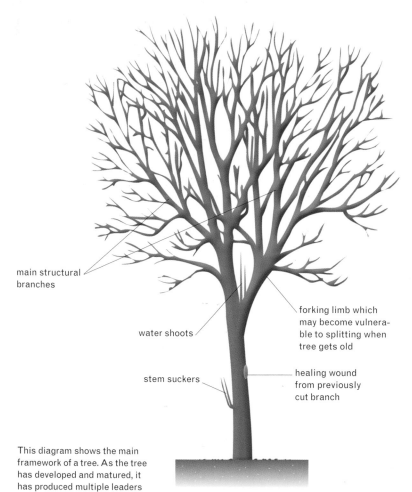

main structural branches

water shoots

stem suckers

forking limb which may become vulnerable to splitting when tree gets old

healing wound from previously cut branch

This diagram shows the main framework of a tree. As the tree has developed and matured, it has produced multiple leaders

Root Network

The reason why a woody plant develops a branched rooting system is to maximize anchorage and exploit the soil for moisture and nutrients. The absorption of water and plant nutrients necessary for growth is the principal function of a root. But it is not so much the root itself that absorbs this goodness, but the microscopic 'root hairs' that come out from the root fibres. The purpose of the root hairs is to provide a larger surface area to provide good absorption. They have a thin cell membrane which also helps. They take in water and the three essential minerals for plant growth: nitrates, phosphates and potassium. As the roots grow larger and older, the root hairs die and the surface becomes corky. New growth will produce more hairs, to expand the roots.

Roots also provide anchorage for the tree or shrub. The depth and extent of the root system are the main factors determining the amount of anchorage involved. Shallow rooted trees, for example, may be blown over with only medium to heavy winds. A deep or 'tap' rooted healthy tree would be able to withstand something much stronger.

To a varying degree, roots also function as a store for accumulated food. This is evident when a tree is removed to ground level but the roots are left in situ. New growth may start, using the food previously manufactured.

So, maintaining a vigorous and widespread root system is essential for maximum growth. A restricted root system, which has perhaps been pruned or cut back, will limit the volume of extension growth at the top of the plant.

Keep an eye on any exposed roots; they reduce the anchorage of the tree

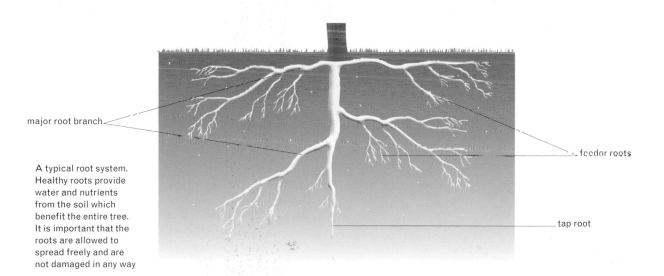

major root branch

feeder roots

tap root

A typical root system. Healthy roots provide water and nutrients from the soil which benefit the entire tree. It is important that the roots are allowed to spread freely and are not damaged in any way

Pruning Techniques

Before the gardener avails himself of the right cutting tools and the correct protective gear, he or she should have a clear understanding of the right and wrong ways to undertake the pruning. Whereabouts on the stem should the cut be made? Does one always need to cut the top growth off an over-vigorous shrub? How does one tackle a congested climber on a wall? And, perhaps most crucially of all, just when is the right time to prune a particular plant? These are all the sorts of questions that need to be addressed before the first cut is made.

Once you have decided (a) which part of the plant needs to be removed, and (b) the best time to do it, you must then make sure that you perform the task in such a way that the plant heals itself as quickly as possible way, and with the minimum risk of infection. Then, of course, you will need to cut to the right buds, with no crushing of the stem. Really, it is not surprising that so many people are put off pruning!

This chapter aims to explain how different pruning techniques can give you the desired results. The techniques employed to prune broadleaved shrubs are entirely different to those for tackling conifers, climbing plants or even palms. The age-old techniques of nicking, notching, bark-ringing and root pruning are now so rarely used, yet could be the answer to your gardening prayers. Pollarding and coppicing will perhaps give your large tree a second chance, before you finally remove it because it is too big. And if you have the desire, the space and the wherewithal, you can create a grand pleached avenue to really impress the neighbours.

Get the Timing Right

It is crucially important to make sure that any pruning carried out is done so at the most appropriate time for the plant in question. Exactly when to undertake routine pruning is determined both by the type of flowering wood the tree or shrub has, and the age of this flowering wood.

When to prune roses?

There are several schools of thought where the pruning of bush roses is concerned. They should certainly be pruned whilst they are dormant – between late autumn and early spring, and if you live in a cooler climate, the later you leave it the better. Some gardeners advocate complete pruning in autumn, but this can run the risk of winter frosts attacking young, tender, premature growths. Others prefer just to tip the roses back in autumn – to avoid autumn and winter winds from rocking and loosening the tall plants in the soil – and save the main pruning until late winter. Neither option is right nor wrong; the eventual decision can be a matter of personal preference and your own experience. See the Pruning Roses section, pages 47–51.

You need to know whereabouts on the stem you should prune before you make the cut

Spring-flowering

Shrubs that carry their blooms in the spring and early summer flower on growth made during the previous year, and are pruned immediately after the flowering is over. The timing here is important, as you need to allow enough time to pass so that the new wood grows and ripens, to maximize the blooming potential in the following year.

Autumn-flowering

On the other hand, late summer and autumn-flowering shrubs carry their blooms on the current season's growth, and are pruned in spring in order to encourage vigorous shoots that will flower on the plants later in the same year.

Cutting growth back to two or three buds first in mid-summer, then again during the winter will help improve next season's fruiting

Some small-leaved shrubs can be cut back with shears once flowering is over

Other considerations

In some cases, other factors must also be taken into account. For example, if evergreens are pruned too early in spring, or too late in summer, they produce new, soft growth that may be damaged by frosts or cold wind. The frost damage may be pruned back to completely healthy wood, making sure you cut to a bud. However, do not do this when more frosts are likely, as the cut will expose buds previously sheltered by the (albeit damaged) stem and foliage, and further frosts are likely to damage these, too.

Then there are some plants that 'bleed' when cut; these should not be pruned in spring, when the pressure of the rising sap could cause excessive bleeding, which might debilitate the plant.

With some trees and shrubs, including apples and pears, flowers are borne on spurs arising from a framework of older wood; the spur wood should be pruned back to the framework, at the appropriate season.

The risk of disease may also be a factor in deciding when to prune a tree, especially a fruit tree. For example, plums are susceptible to a number of different infections (most importantly silver leaf disease), which gain entry through pruning wounds, especially if made in winter. Therefore undertake such pruning when plants are in active growth.

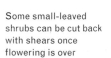

Making Cuts

The most important rule when it comes to making a pruning cut is that the pruned stem must always terminate with a bud, where buds are visible. Additionally, the cut must be as reasonably close to the bud as possible without damaging it.

If using secateurs, place the blades a fraction above the bud. With a pruning knife, however, start the cut on the side opposite to the bud but at approximately the same level. Then draw the knife towards the bud, but in a direction slanting upwards, so that the shoot is severed slightly above it.

Snags

If a cut is made between two buds, but the tip of the pruned shoot is a long distance from the bud below it, there is nothing to draw the sap up the shoot, so it will gradually die back. One is then left with a 'snag' – the gardener's term for a dead piece of wood resulting from incorrect pruning.

Snags are frequently seen in the fork of two closely growing shoots, where the person pruning has not taken the trouble to remove the centre piece of wood cleanly. A useful tool here is a joiner's padsaw, which has a very narrow blade.

Make a straight cut when you are dealing with opposite buds

Cut diagonally away from the bud or stem in order to help rainwater run off the surface of the wound

Bud angles

In an ideal situation you should be cutting to a bud that is pointing in the right direction. It is important to keep the centre of any growing plant as 'open' as possible, in order that the sun can ripen wood in the inner parts of the plant, and also that air can circulate freely here. Therefore, when pruning, you should where possible prune to a bud that is facing 'outwards' from the centre of the plant.

The angle, or slope, of the cut is important, as this helps rainwater to run off the surface. You should not, however, make the angle of cut so oblique as to expose an excessive surface area for the entry of frost or disease.

Removing a Large Branch

Most gardeners who possess mature and established trees will need to remove branches occasionally. If a branch is too long, or perhaps too thick to cut easily with secateurs or loppers, it should really be sawn off. This should be carried out in manageable stages, mainly so that you can remove each section of branch from the site with relative ease (wood is heavy!).

Common mistakes

When pruning stems people often commit the following errors:

- making the cut too far from the bud, therefore leaving a 'snag'
- making the cut too close to the bud, which can damage tissue near to the bud
- sloping away from the bud at too sharp an angle
- sloping towards the bud
- a torn, damaged or ragged cut is perfect for the entry of pests and diseases as it will not heal effectively

1

2

After removing the sections you should eventually be left with a stub 30–45cm (12–18in) long. Do not leave the stub. It is unsightly and can be dangerous. It will invariably die off anyway, and it will then make the perfect entry point for pests and diseases.

3

Avoiding splits

For smaller branches, you should be able to remove cleanly the remaining stub simply by making a cut from above (1). With a larger branch, however, it is a good idea to make an undercut (2), by perhaps as much as a third of the diameter of the branch, before making the final cut from above (3). The result of failing to undercut a branch in this way will be that the stump falls under its own weight before the final downward cut is completed, and this can easily tear a long, jagged wound in the bark on the trunk as it falls. Significant damage can be caused to the tree, and it may take a long time to callus and heal.

Paring back

At the end of the final cut, the stub should fall to the ground, more or less level, leaving a raised, rough-sawn 'wound' on the tree (4). When a large branch has been removed it is wise to pare the wound to a smooth surface. A sharp pruning knife is generally used for this purpose. The result will be more pleasing to the eye, it will encourage the formation of a neater callus and it will make a better surface – if this is your desire – for the application of a wound sealant (see page 25 regarding the use of wound sealant).

4

Root Pruning

This is usually carried out when a tree or shrub makes too much growth and consequently produces little or no flower and fruit. In more cases than not, the root system has run amok, so must be restrained in order that there may be a corresponding slackening off in the vigour of the top growth. Winter is the best time to undertake root pruning.

Young trees

With an over-vigorous but young tree, perhaps up to five years old, the best course of action is to transplant it. The very act of digging it up and planting it again will be sufficient to cut the roots and check the rate of growth.

Older trees

Older trees will not transplant well, so root pruning will have to take a different form. Take out a trench, some 1.5m (5ft) from the stem. As the thick roots become exposed you will need to use a pruning saw to cut through them.

It is, perhaps, a good idea to avoid giving the plant too big a check in its growth, so divide the operation into two halves. One 180° side of the tree can be pruned one winter, leaving the other side until the following winter.

Which trees?

Root pruning is practised on a wide range of fruit trees, but particularly apples, apricots, cherries, figs, grapevines, nectarines, peaches, pears and plums, as well as trees and shrubs grown for their ornamental value. The most likely subjects are apples and pears when grown as cordons or espaliers, and cherries and plums when cultivated as fan-trained trees.

Once you have finished pruning it is important to refill the trench as soon as possible, so that valuable moisture is not lost from the soil, and when replacing the soil make sure you thoroughly firm it in. Backfill methodically, layer-by-layer, and firm with a rammer, your boot or even the spade handle. Firm ground encourages production of the fibrous thin roots that are so important for taking up water and nutrients to the top part of the plant.

TIP

It is important to make every cut as cleanly as possible. Jagged cuts or tears result in rotting, whereas clean cuts can lead to the formation of new, fibrous roots.

Pruning roots before planting

An alternative method of pruning roots is to cut them back before the subject is planted. For example, when planting out a rose bush normally the hole dug to accommodate the roots is circular, or at least of a regular shape. Rose roots, however, can be long and irregularly shaped. Some judicious cutting back to about 23cm (9in) of the stem with a pair of secateurs will make planting much easier, and will perhaps shock the plant in to throwing out some new shoots.

Needless to say, while you have the plant in your hand, you should also remove any damaged or diseased roots.

Bark Ringing

The sort of excessive vigour that can be dealt with by root pruning (see above) can also be checked by an operation called bark-ringing. The object is to interrupt the downward flow of sugars and similar foodstuffs within the plant. This effectively checks the roots and the rate of growth slows down. Spring is the best season to do it.

Although bark-ringing can be applied to many ornamental trees, it is only of real value where fruit trees are concerned, apples and pears being the most suitable. Plums, cherries and other stone fruits tend to object to the interference.

To carry out the operation, use a sharp knife to remove a strip of bark some 6mm (1/4in) wide, extending the strip three quarters of the way around the trunk. Ensure that you do not remove a continuous circle of bark around the trunk, as this would probably kill the tree. Leave at least 2.5cm (1in) of the ring uncut to allow for a modicum of sap flow.

The wound must be left open for as little time as possible. Quickly wrap around the circle a double or triple layer of masking or adhesive tape, followed by a smear of petroleum jelly along the edges of the tape. This will exclude the air, and the possible risk of pest and disease entry, and will also assist healing.

Nicking

This really goes hand-in-hand with bark-ringing and the next method described: notching. All three are concerned with stopping or deflecting the sap flow, and in this particular case it will help to curtail an over-vigorous plant or part of a plant. For this particular operation, cut a nick – a small triangular shaped cut in the bark – just below a bud. The bud's development will be weakened, if not stopped completely. The theory is to produce a weaker shoot and in practice this works reasonably well. Spring is the right season to carry out these operations.

Notching

Here the aim is to cut out a similar wedge of bark with a sharp pruning knife, but this time just above the bud. The bud should, and usually is, stimulated into growth, and this works well where, for example, a dormant bud is required to grow. It is more likely to be practised on a fruit tree which is being trained in a specific way, and where branches are needed in specific places. Notching is best done in the dormant season; late winter for preference.

Pollarding

'Pollarding' is the term used to describe the repeated severe pruning of a tree or shrub. 'Coppicing' – a similar but slightly different technique – involves cutting off the parent plant at or about ground level.

Both techniques are sometimes practised for purely decorative purposes, although the plant is not particularly attractive immediately after being pruned in these ways!

Fast-growing trees or shrubs in a garden situation, such as forms of the sweet gum (*Eucalyptus* spp.), can be treated by pollarding or coppicing, in order to keep them to manageable proportions.

Pollarding is often carried out in order to keep the head of a large tree within manageable proportions. Every few years a gang of workers will reduce drastically the heads of the trees, to almost ridiculous proportions. However, within a few months the new leaves will conceal the ugly shapes, and after a season the trees will be quite presentable.

Pollarding is a fairly drastic measure, but it will benefit a badly over-grown tree

Pleaching

Pleaching – the word comes from an old French term meaning 'to braid' or 'interweave' – is a technique in which plant training, hedging, pruning and topiary come together to allow the gardener in effect to 'crochet' with living trees.

'Pleached walks', whereby the branches of an avenue of trees, such as lime (Tilia), are knitted together to form a green tunnel, frequently impress visitors to stately gardens. The Elizabethans were the most enthusiastic creators of such secluded walks; the features were a form of status symbol, indicating the number of workers the owner of the land was able to keep. The Victorians hastened the process a little by

Pleachable trees

Not only limes, but whitethorn (Crataegus), hornbeam (Carpinus), beech (Fagus), holly (Ilex), willow (Salix) and some fruit trees have been pleached successfully down the centuries. In reality, most trees that tolerate clipping are suitable. Using forms of beech with varying leaf colours, mainly purple, green and yellow, for example, a striking tapestry effect can be created. In winter, when there are no leaves on the pleached trees, the closely interwoven branches have an ornamental value of their own.

using ornate iron frames over which to weave the tree branches to make bowers.

Although this sort of feature is perfectly suited to the more traditional, perhaps older, and certainly larger garden, it is questionable as to whether one would be appropriate in an average 'back' garden.

Basic pleaching

Creating your own pleached feature will take several years and a considerable amount of work: you need patience and perseverance! All sorts of effects can be achieved over time, from a thick hedge raised on stilts to a green tunnel, an arbour, a bower or a 'cave'.

First plant several trees in a row some 2.4m (8ft) apart and allow them to grow naturally until they become firmly established. Then lop off each tree at the same height. Next, you will need to make a connecting frame of wires or bamboo canes, which is positioned so that new growth can be trained along it until the branches interweave – a process that will take at least three years. Cut off all shoots that grow out of line.

The frame may be positioned vertically along the row of trees; therefore two frames would be needed for an avenue, one each side. Alternatively, a frame could be constructed and placed overhead, so that the branches meet over the top of the walkway. Clearly, the structure should be soundly built, anchored and braced so as to ensure the safety of those who are walking underneath.

Creating a pleached avenue will take a good few years to achieve the desired affect

Renovation Pruning of Shrubs

Fortunately, most vigorous shrubs respond well to hard pruning for the purpose of renovation. This means that if you move house and inherit a neglected hardy hybrid rhododendron, common laurel (*Prunus laurocerasus*), French hybrid lilac (Syringa) or a mock orange (Philadelphus), or through some fault of your own you have allowed such a shrub to become overgrown, with crowded stems, accumulated dead wood and therefore few, or small flowers – all is not lost. As long as the shrub is healthy, pruning it hard is likely to be the most effective way of giving it a new lease of life.

Make the distinction here between renovation pruning and coppicing/pollarding (see page 35). The former should only be carried out when the plant has been neglected, and hopefully therefore just once during its life. The latter techniques, on the other hand, are carried out on a regular basis, perhaps annually or every two or three years.

There are clear advantages to renovating through pruning, rather than digging out an overgrown shrub entirely: the cost of a new plant is avoided, and a mature-sized, well-shaped plant can be the result in a relatively short time. The plant might not look good at first, but growth during the year following pruning should be rapid.

Renovation pruning in practice

Hard pruning to renovate is simple. Cut all weak shoots down to ground level and prune back other main shoots to approximately 30cm (1ft) above the ground. With evergreen subjects this is done in the spring, just as growth commences, but in winter in the case of deciduous shrubs.

Forms of Deutzia and Philadelphus should be renovated over a two-year period, half the plant tackled each year. This avoids too great a shock to the plants' systems, and allows the shrubs to continue to look moderately

attractive throughout the renovation process. Feeding, mulching and watering must also be carefully attended to, especially in the first season following pruning.

The shrub's response will be to produce several shoots from each of the shortened shoots. Formative pruning, with the aim of restoring the shrub's characteristic habit, should now begin. Remove all of the weakest shoots, leaving only two or three of the strongest shoots per stump. These shoots will now produce the new framework.

A straggly, overgrown and generally neglected shrub, or shrubbery, can be given an amazing makeover with careful restorative pruning (see illustration below)

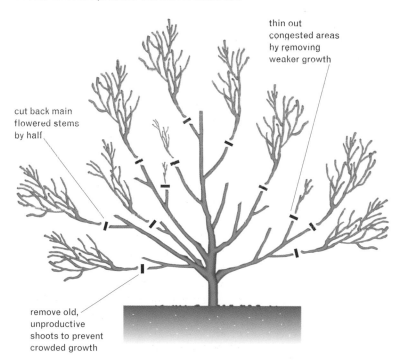

thin out congested areas by removing weaker growth

cut back main flowered stems by half

remove old, unproductive shoots to prevent crowded growth

Pruning & Training Conifers

Removing a double leader with secateurs will help maintain the balance of the plant

With almost every conifer there will come a time when it will need to be pruned, either to keep it to a reasonable size, or simply for shape. Not all conifers improve as they age; they can become unbalanced, or they just get too big. If you have a small garden, then you should be prepared to prune as need be.

Sadly, unlike broadleaved trees, conifers (with the exception of yew) do not regenerate readily from mature wood as there are few or no dormant buds present in the older branches. Any pruning of mature conifers should be restricted to removing entirely dead or dying branches. Attempts to reduce mature conifers in height normally leave unsatisfactory and frequently ugly, mutilated plants that are best removed.

Columnar conifers

With trees of columnar shape, such as the false cypress (*Chamaecyparis* spp.) or arborvitaes (*Thuja* spp.), it is a good idea when a tree is young to reduce the number of leading shoots to just one, and then to trim it back lightly all over. Do this in spring or mid-summer, and repeat the process every two years. Eventually the density of the tree will be increased, but its width reduced.

Firs and pines

Tipping back a dwarf conifer will keep the plant balanced and healthy and will encourage new growth

The basic growth pattern of firs (*Abies* spp.) and pines (*Pinus* spp.) is for a single central

TIP

Grafted conifers
Sometimes the conifers bought from a garden centre are grafted on to a different conifer rooting stock. Occasionally the leader can be over-taken by one of the side shoots, and this can unbalance the plant. Prune back the competing leader half-way, and shorten the other side shoots so that they do not take its place.

Conifers for hedging

Several conifers such as yew (*Taxus baccata*), Chamaecyparis and Thuja, make excellent hedging plants (see pages 52–55). Perhaps the most famous conifer for hedging is the Leyland cypress (x *Cupressocyparis leylandii*). Mature specimens can extend by 1.2m (4ft) per year, and it is all too easy to allow a hedge to get quickly out of control. It is important, therefore, to ensure that from a very early stage in the life of the hedge, that it is clipped annually every spring, and given a further trimming in late summer if it really needs attention. Leaving the hedge to grow to an enormous size before hacking it back drastically is likely to result in an ugly mess, since the trees will not regenerate from old wood.

leader to grow with branches radiating from them, and at fairly regular intervals along its length. The shoots should be left to grow naturally and only if they are damaged will any pruning be necessary as the plants will basically take care of themselves.

Sometimes the leader, or the terminal bud, dies and usually one or more shoots from the uppermost shoots will begin to replace it naturally. As soon as you spot the need for a replacement leader, vertically train the best-placed shoot of the upper whorl, and at the same time cut out completely any competing shoots.

Pruning Palms & Palm-like Plants

Generally, the leaves of palms (and palm-like plants such as Cordyline and Yucca), should only be removed when they are dead. However, you could make an exception for such palms as the Chusan or windmill palm (*Trachycarpus fortunei*). Its green, healthy leaves can remain on the trunk until they reach down to ground level; allow them to continue growing and the plant will begin to look unsightly. The leaves are often, therefore, removed from the lower branches of mature specimens. From a half to two thirds of the bottom, leaves are normally pruned.

Restricting size

You may remove excess and older canes of multi-stemmed palms periodically. However, you should never cut the head off a single-trunk palm: because there are no growth buds lower down on the trunk, this will prevent it from ever generating new leaves and, in time, will cause it to die.

For this reason is it difficult to restrict a palm to size simply by pruning. When a palm outgrows its allotted space you have a limited supply of options. If it is in a pot, in a conservatory for example, you can either

Palm pruning tips

- After a palm has flowered, the bracts can be cut 5–8cm (2–3in) away from the trunk.
- Old leaves should also be cut 5–8cm (2–3in) from the trunk. Yuccas, cordylines and phormiums all need to have their old leaves removed. If old leaves do not pull away easily, use sharp secateurs to cut them off.
- Remove spent flower spikes by cutting as far down their spikes as possible; a pair of secateurs is usually the best tool for the job.
- Damaged leaves are best pruned when their foliage has dried out and become shrivelled.
- Many palms produce a fibrous covering over the trunk; this forms protection against the cold, so should be left in place.

plant it out in the garden (as long as the palm is sufficiently hardy to survive outdoors), or you can give it away to someone who can accommodate it, or you can throw it away. If a palm is outgrowing its garden situation, the latter two options are the only ones available!

Control the spread of suckering palms, such as the Mediterranean or European palm (*Chamaerops humilis*), by using a saw to cut unwanted suckers from the base of the plant.

Be careful when you are handling spiky plants and wear stout gloves if in doubt.

Use secateurs to cut back the old leaves of palms. The trunk should also be tidied up regularly

Removing the flowerhead of a yucca will keep the plant looking tidier and more architectural

Pruning & Training Climbers

The value of growing climbing plants is clear: they grow vertically, and can therefore clothe an ugly wall or fence; their climbing growth adds a different dimension to planting; they are very space efficient for a garden of restricted size. Arguably, climbers are of most use in a small garden, where the extra dimension of colour and greenery can be appreciated even more.

If you do not have an expanse of wall or fence up which to grow climbers, there are free-standing structures you can use, such as arches, tripods, pillars, poles, medium to large-sized trees, or even multi-legged pergolas, obelisks, gazebos and, if you have the space and the pocket, summerhouses and other garden buildings.

A question of support

It is normally best to choose the climber that is most suitable for the particular site. On a bare wall, for example, only a climber that

Stout, heavy climbing plants like this wisteria need substantial support wherever they are climbing

Pruning

TIP If climbing plants are going to be grown against wooden buildings or fences that will need painting from time to time, it is a good idea to fix trellis panels with hinges, so that they can be swung away as and when necessary.

How climbers climb

Essentially, climbers are plants with weak stems that take themselves up towards the light by various means:

- by twining stems, as in honeysuckle (*Lonicera periclymenum*)
- by twining leaf stalks, as in clematis
- by roots produced from the stems, that stick to the support, as in ivy (Hedera)
- by tendrils, as in vines (Vitis)
- by pads on tendrils, that stick to the support, as in Virginia creeper (Parthenocissus)
- by thorns, which hook on to the support, as in climbing roses
- by lax stems that 'flop' over structures such as rocks, trees or shrubs

sticks itself to its support can be used. However, if the wall is supporting a trellis or a series of parallel wires, almost any kind of climber can be grown.

Parallel wires These are the easiest form of support to install and maintain. The wire should be of a sufficiently heavy gauge to support a weight of stems and leaves for a prolonged period of time. They should be fixed to the wall, horizontally, some 30cm (12in) or less apart. Use eyebolts and strainers at each end to keep them taut. If you do not have a suitable wall, the parallel wires can be set between free-standing stout and well-secured posts; the advantage with this is that you can attend to the climbing plants from both sides of the wire.

Trelliswork Before a trellis panel is securely fixed to the wall, it should be painted or treated with a wood preservative. The thickness of the timber used depends on the type of climber it will have to support. Strong climbers, such as wisteria, produce

Tie in the stems of climbing plants to trellis with green wire or string. It will help support them as they grow

TIP

Climbers that use supports, such as honeysuckle and clematis, can be pruned more thoroughly if they are first detached from the supports to make cutting and clearing of the prunings easier.

heavy stems, so strong supports are necessary. Metal trelliswork can be used as long as it has been painted and galvanized to prevent rusting.

Trees Mature, large trees make wonderful supports for strong-growing climbers. The tree could even be dead; in fact, if a tree has died and removing it is troublesome, hiding it under a climber effectively gives it a new lease of life. You may need to plant the climber some distance from the bowl of the trunk. If so, insert a cane or use vertical wires to take the climber's stems up into the branches of the tree. If the tree is alive, and depending on its size, you may be advised to choose medium-strength climbers, such as Clematis, as opposed to the stronger Wisteria or Vitis. Whatever you opt for, be prepared to be ruthless with the climber at pruning time, so that the supporting tree is not smothered.

Poles, posts and pillars These sorts of free-standing structures may require some wire, eyebolts, hooks or nails placed strategically to assist the climbers on their way up. Wooden poles and posts should be treated with wood preservative, at least at their bases and, for security, should be set into concrete under the ground. Metal poles should be painted or galvanized to prevent rusting. You should really grow weaker climbers on these structures, or at least make sure you prune each year so that there is never too much growth for the structure to support.

Pergolas Because these structures are multi-legged and braced, they can support strong climbers. You may find that as the climbers grow over the top of the pergola, they will cause a reduction in light at the footings of the posts. This, in turn, can cause lower leaves to fall. One way to avoid having bare stems halfway up the pergola is to plant selected small climbers; they will conceal the bare stems and provide colour lower down.

Pruning climbers

The same rules apply to the pruning of established climbers as for shrubs (see Get the timing right, page 31). Prune climbers flowering on previous season's wood after being in flower. Remove shoots that have flowered or cut them back to where new growth is developing, then thin out the remaining growth.

Cut back any stems growing away from the wall in order to reduce the weight of the plant

Climbers which flower on current season's growths can be cut hard back to a framework during the winter; more often than not they are cut to ground level. Hard pruning like this will delay flowering, so to extend the flowering season you could just lightly trim some shoots, and cut back the rest. Train in new shoots as they develop, keeping only enough to completely furnish the support; any surplus stems should be cut away.

If the main stems of your climber are old and bare, cut them out completely and replace them with some of the younger stems – either shoots growing from ground level or from low down on the old stems.

Snap dead or faded flowers off between forefingers and thumb

Deadheading

Deadheading, or the removal of faded flowerheads, is essential if you are to maintain quality and quantity of flower. It applies to almost every flowering plant, be it a shrub, perennial, flowering bulb or even a bedding plant, whereby the removal of faded flowers prolongs the flowering season. In the case of woody plants and perennials, if the old flowers are allowed to stay and form seed, few flower buds are likely to be produced the following year.

The removal of larger flowerheads can be quickly done by hand, once the knack is learned; small trusses can be snapped off between fingers and thumbs. Certain garden rhododendrons have long flower stalks and the seed capsules are set up well above the leaves. Cut these off with a small pair of scissors.

Deadheading roses

For some roses, deadheading can be combined with reducing the height of flowering stems during late summer or early autumn. With a pair of secateurs cut off 23–30cm (9–12in) of the fading flowerhead. It is often recommended to reduce the height of shoots by this much to prevent the plant being rocked about by the high autumn winds.

This method applies to floribundas (cluster flowered bush roses) and hybrid teas (large flowered roses). Faded flowers on first year roses and those on most shrub roses should be removed with very little stem. Do not deadhead those varieties grown for their decorative hips, as this will spoil the fruiting process.

Pruning Reverted Growth

'Reversion' most often occurs when a variegated tree or shrub suddenly produces a normal green-leaved shoot. Such 'reverted' shoots should be cut off as soon as they are seen, since having the normal amount of green pigment (chlorophyll) in their leaves means they will be more vigorous and will rapidly dominate the shrub.

The same problem may arise with cultivars that have been bred for their finely cut or divided leaves; shoots carrying the more plain, 'usual' kind of leaf should be removed.

Grafted plants, or even plants like Eucalyptus or *Picea abies* 'Gregoryana' that retain their juvenile foliage, can be prone to reverted shoots.

Remove green shoots from variegated plants to improve the way they look and to keep the plant in the best of health

Pruning Suckers

Suckers occur naturally on a host of garden trees and shrubs, and frequently from the rootstocks of grafted plants (it is perhaps in the rose border that this most commonly applies, see below). When growing out from a plant's roots, suckers should be traced back to the original point of growth and then cut off. The surrounding tissue should also be pared away, so as to remove dormant buds nearby.

Suckers should always be removed, as they are both unsightly and an unnecessary drain on the plant's energies. Apples, pears and cherries are particularly prone to suckering in the fruit patch, while poplars (Populus), limes (Tilia), Robinia, lilacs (Syringa), Sumach, Symphoricarpos and many weeping trees and shrubs are likely to sucker in the ornamental garden.

Rose suckers

These are generally easily recognized. The leaves of rose suckers are usually light green, rounder than the true leaves, and quite distinct, especially when among roses with dark green or bronzy leaves.

TIP

Good nurserymen clean off suckers before displaying or sending out their plants, but mistakes can, and do, occur. Therefore, inspect the subject before you plant it, and remove cleanly any knob-like shoot on the roots.

When removing suckers from rose bushes, trace the sucker back to the original point of growth and make the cut there

43

With standard and half-standard roses on a wide-spreading rootstock, such as *Rosa rugosa*, suckers may appear some distance away from the plants, and this can lead to some confusion. However, they generally originate just under the soil surface, and can be traced back for removal.

When suckers occur on stems of standard roses, they are best rubbed when young.

Disbudding & Pinching

There are a number of miscellaneous ways in which the gardener can inhibit excessively vigorous growth, or encourage the formation of new growth where in the past the plant has been shy.

Pinching

Most gardeners do a great deal of their pruning by 'pinching' off new growth that is not wanted. It may be to encourage the plant to be more bushy, with more lateral stems low down – pinching the leader and/or top growths off will stimulate dormant buds into growth. Perhaps, also, a growth may be heading off in the wrong direction: pinching, with the thumb and forefinger can remove the terminal bud.

You can nip out the tips of many plants by simply squeezing them between finger and thumb

Disbudding

Many flowering and fruiting plants if left to their own devices would bring forth lots of small and medium-sized blooms. So, if you want to encourage them to reach their full potential, pinch off most of the buds when still small, leaving perhaps only one on each stem. Florists and growers disbud carnations (Dianthus), chrysanthemums, dahlias, roses and so on, because sometimes one giant blossom is more desirable than a lot of smaller ones.

It might seem ironic, but regular disbudding of some plants will improve the display of flowers

Cutting Back Perennials

Most herbaceous perennial plants should be cut back in the autumn, but there are exceptions (see box, right). Cutting back is necessary to stop dead top growth falling to the ground and rotting on the soil, creating the perfect breeding ground for pests and diseases. It also allows the gardener good access to the soil to aerate it with a hoe or fork, and to clean away weeds and debris.

Start cutting back perennials once autumn frosts have brought an end to the border's growth and flowering. Choose a day

Perennials NOT to cut

Not all herbaceous perennials should be cut back in autumn. Do not cut back plantain lilies (Hosta) or elephant's ears (Bergenia). Leaves of the former will rot naturally, and can be removed at the end of the year. Old leaves and stems can be removed from the latter when required. Leave alone, too, the smaller border plants such as violas and primulas.

Plants grown for their winter flowers, such as hellebores – the plants better known as Lenten and Christmas roses – should be cut back after flowering, usually around late spring. Replacement growths, that will carry blooms the following winter, should be visible by this time, and these should be left.

Finally, there are some plants that produce seeds which birds find useful during the winter months; these can be left. They include bramble (Rubus), cornflower (Centaurea), globe thistle (Echinops), golden rod (Solidago), honesty (Lunaria), Michaelmas daisy (*Aster novi-belgii*), sunflower (Helianthus) and yarrow (Achillea).

when there is no frost, but the ground is damp. Use secateurs, shears or loppers to cut most plants down to about 10cm (4in) from the soil.

Start at the back of the bed or border and, as you work forwards, fork over the top few inches of soil, taking care not to disturb the roots of the plants.

In colder parts, the top growth can be left on some of the more tender plants. This will protect the crowns from the worst of the winter weather, but you will need to cut the dead stems away before growth starts again in spring.

Ornamental Grasses

As with perennials, ornamental grasses, rushes and sedges usually need cutting back annually. However, the timing of the annual trim will depend on local conditions. For the more tender species this is generally to be preferred after winter has passed, as the dying or wilting foliage offers some protection against frost and cold. An early spring trim will also encourage quick renewal of the vegetative growth. With the hardier and more robust grasses, late autumn is acceptable unless the garden is in a particularly cold spot.

Some of the herbaceous grasses take on an appealing parchment-like or coloured hue during late summer and autumn, and if this is to be enjoyed they should be left undisturbed until the early spring, before cleaning up.

Trimming grasses

As with lawn grasses, it is the newly formed growth of ornamental grasses that has a deeper intensity of leaf colour. When trimming over the hump-like and ground covering grasses, be careful not to damage the soft tips of young growth. The job is best carried out using a pair of sharp garden shears. Make a first shear some 30cm (12in) off the ground and then clear the area of trimming so that you can see into the centre of the plant. Now you can trim a little closer, or to make a more rounded clump. Be careful not to destroy the crown of the plant when cutting down to this extent.

Cutting back bamboos

Bamboos do not generally need much in the way of pruning. Use loppers, or a saw in tough cases, to remove any damaged or discoloured canes; this is best done in spring. If a clump has become too dense, it can be thinned (in late spring or summer).

Most species of bamboo can be renovated by cutting all canes to the ground, and for some forms 'coppicing' will produce better-looking canes and foliage. For example, the

Many grasses with old, browning foliage (top) benefit from a thorough cutting back with sharp garden shears (bottom)

This bamboo – *Phyllostachys nigra* – will benefit from occasional thinning but does not require much else

golden variegated bamboo (*Arundinaria auricoma*) will display its brightest foliage after it has been cut to ground level; the fresh new growths produce the most golden of variegated leaves.

Flaming pampas!

Instead of cutting back the old, dead leaves of pampas grass (*Cortaderia selloana*), it is a common practice to set light to them. The act replicates the phenomenon that happens in the plants' natural habitat in South America, where whole swathes of prairie catch alight periodically and so 'cleanse' plants of the old, unwanted foliage. However, there is a danger of destroying the crown if the flames get a hold. It is therefore wise to have water at hand to prevent flames burning the crown (from where new growth will emerge).

Be particularly careful when handling the leaves of pampas grass, as the stiff, serrated edges are very sharp and can cut the skin.

Pruning Roses

Most beginner gardeners know that, regardless of what other plants might be growing, it is the roses that will, at some stage, need pruning. A majority of gardens possess one or two rose bushes and without an annual trim, these plants will soon become lanky and unsightly, with just a few feeble flowers.

Although we will be showing you here how to prune bush roses in the orthodox way, there is an increasing school of thought that suggests these plants end up just as well if they are cut back in a haphazard way – say with a hedge trimmer. Certainly, evidence is now pointing to the reduced need to cut to a bud, and hence ensuring that the cut is not too close, nor that the slope of cut is too flat or steep. The decision as to which way to prune is yours, but at least if you wish to do it in the old-fashioned way, the information you need is here.

Many people herald the rose as the 'flower of England'. It certainly has a long English heritage, with the old-fashioned roses of York and Lancaster leading the way. But the Rosa genus is huge, its origins being on a worldwide scale: India, China and Japan have a long connection with shrub

Floribundas, or cluster-flowered bush roses, are one of the most popular forms of this plant

roses, as do the Ancient Greek and Roman civilizations. Australia, New Zealand and South America are perhaps the most notable areas where no native species have so far been found. Today, the breeding of roses takes place all over the world, and new cultivars are introduced to commerce every year.

The most popular group of roses are the large-flowered bush roses, or hybrid teas. Second to these are the cluster-flowered bush roses, or floribundas. These bear their flowers in clusters, and several blooms open at a time in each cluster. Floribundas were not widely grown until the 1950s, but newer still are the miniatures, which can be grown in tubs and rock gardens, or grown as edging for flowerbeds or even as temporary indoor pot plants. Then there are shrub and species roses (which actually need far less in the way of pruning), climbers, ramblers and ground-cover roses.

The rose is an acquired taste; some people seeming to dislike them intensely. It is true that they generally need looking after – pruning, feeding, mulching and pest and disease control – but they do reward this effort with masses of colour and the scent given off by some forms is a bonus!

Shrub roses are particularly rewarding with their flowers in early summer; many also produce red hips in autumn

Garden Hybrid Bush Roses

How to prune bush roses is a matter of some debate (see page 30), but they should certainly be pruned while they are dormant – between late autumn and early spring.

Hybrid teas

The most popular group of roses for decorating the summer garden are the hybrid tea large-flowered bush roses. The flowers are shapely and they sit on long, strong stems. There is a bewildering range of colours available, true blue being about the only absentee. The fragrance is usually medium or strong, and the blooms are perfect for exhibiting in local competition shows, or cutting for indoor decoration; if cut at the right stage, they last well in water.

The aim when pruning is to encourage the development of strong basal growths and to form an open-centred plant with an evenly spaced system of branches.

When planting a new hybrid tea rose, immediately cut all of its shoots back to around 15cm (6in) from the ground. Always cut to an outward facing bud.

By early summer new shoots will have developed; during late summer or early autumn tip back the flowered stems (1) and cut out any soft, unripe shoots.

The following winter start the annual routine pruning: first cut out dead and diseased wood (2), and remove any inward-growing or crossing stems, then cut back each shoot to between 15–23cm (6–9in) from ground level (or more for the less vigorous stems).

1

2

Floribundas

Second in popularity to the hybrid teas are the floribundas. These bear their flowers in clusters, and several blooms open at a time in each cluster. Individually the blooms are not so spectacular as the hybrid tea, but in a bedding display they are unrivalled. They more or less flower continually throughout summer and autumn, whereas with hybrid teas there are distinct flushes of bloom during the summer months.

Floribundas are more vigorous than the hybrid teas, so generally they should be pruned less severely.

Carry out the pruning at the same time as for hybrid teas, by cutting back all growths to three or five buds from the base. In terms of length this will be around 23–25cm (9–10in) from the ground.

Remove any suckers found, and cut out all weak, damaged or moribund shoots.

At the end of the growing season, during mid-autumn, it is a good idea to tip back the main flowering stems, and completely remove any soft, sappy shoots.

TIP

In the main, roses are grafted or budded, but occasionally they will be raised on their own roots; this is more often the case with climbers, shrub or species roses raised from cuttings or seed. In all of these, shoots coming from beneath the ground can be allowed to grow, for they will not be suckers.

Climbers & Ramblers

Many people are confused about the differences between climbers and ramblers. The former have larger flowers but smaller trusses and stiffer stems, while the latter have long pliable stems and bear trusses of smallish flowers. If you want to cover a wall or screen, it is usually better to choose a climber. Ramblers can be used effectively to trail along the soil as ground cover or trailed through old trees.

Climbing roses

Flowers are carried on the framework of mature wood, which should be maintained for as long as possible. Here we can see a rose growing on a pillar. The advice given is the same, regardless of the type of structure the rose is climbing up:

Set the post or pillar in the ground before planting the rose; this will avoid unnecessary disturbance to the roots. Also, undertake any root pruning at this stage, and prune any weak growth or damaged stems.

The first summer flowers will appear on laterals from the old wood, and new growth will have developed from the base of the plant. Deadhead all faded flower trusses.

In late autumn or early winter cut back the flowered laterals and some new shoots to maintain the plant's symmetry. Regular pruning at this time should also consist of cutting out weak and damaged wood and, importantly, tying in the new shoots.

Rambler roses

These are, perhaps, more colourful than climbers at certain times, but there is only one flush of bloom. Growth is extremely vigorous, but the leaves need regular spraying to combat mildew, to which these roses are prone. Here we can see an established rambler, supported by horizontal wires. The flowers are carried on new wood, so each year the old wood should be completely removed.

Pruning a trained rambling rose effectively involves making cuts at the positions denoted by the red cut lines in the illustration above. If the plant requires substantial thinning, cut several main stems at the base, as indicated

At planting time, preferably during autumn or late winter, remove completely a few of the plant's weakest shoots, and cut back the rest of the growths to 23–38cm (9–15in).

In spring new shoots will start to develop; as soon as they are of a suitable size train them into place on the horizontal support wires. A few flowers will appear in the first year on lateral shoots.

Immediately after flowering, cut out the flowered shoots so that the new basal shoots can be tied in to place.

In the second and third years, when there should be masses more flowers, repeat the same technique of removing spent growth and tying in the new.

Tying shoots into a post will keep both climbing and rambling roses supported and will assist them in growing upwards

Use secateurs to selectively prune overlong stems on shrub roses

Shrub Roses

This is a surprisingly large group of plants. They are divided into species roses, modern shrub roses and old-fashioned (or old garden) roses. The latter group are further divided into groups with names like the Damasks, Moss roses, Bourbons and Gallicas: they are all extremely rewarding during early summer and again in autumn if they produce bright hips. They are particularly at home in informal gardens and where their graceful, perhaps arching stems may have a little more room to grow upwards and outwards.

It is often recommended to leave a shrub or species rose unpruned, as if to grow naturally and unrestricted. This will usually last well for a few years, but the plant will not, in the long run, supply the gardener with the optimum display of blooms.

The key to pruning a shrub rose is to develop a framework of sturdy shoots. Cut a small number of the oldest branches each year to leave strong new shoots to take their place, which will effectively renew the framework, and at the same time aim to achieve an open-centred plant. Regularly deadhead the faded blooms – unless the

plant is grown for its display of autumn and winter hips.

Once a year tip back all vigorous shoots and laterals.

Miniature & Patio Roses

Miniature roses did not become popular until the 1970s. Most are 38cm (15in) high, or under, and both flowers and leaves are small, yet in proportion with the rest of the plant.

The pruning of miniatures is basically similar to that recommended for hybrid teas, although one should not cut back newly planted miniatures too drastically.

Occasionally, over-vigorous shoots are thrown up, which will spoil the overall look of the plant. Remove these entirely when pruning, so that the plant has a proper balanced framework throughout the growing season.

As usual, deadheading is an important task, but do not be too severe.

Cut out weak shoots and tip back the stronger stems to about 10–15cm (4–6in) from the ground.

Patio and polyantha roses are newer still, having been introduced to commerce within the past two decades. They are essentially small floribundas, and are pruned in a similar way, though on a smaller scale. Try to avoid damaging the leaves of all these smaller rose types, as it is both unsightly and a severe amount of damage can debilitate a plant.

Miniature roses are pruned in much the same way as their larger cousins, but be careful with young plants

> **TIP**
>
> The number of shrub roses is vast, and includes many species with varying habits of growth and flowering. Most grow naturally by a system of replacement of the older flowering branches by young ones. The type of pruning depends largely on the vigour of the rose, and the extent of its ability to replace old wood.

Standard Roses

Long-stemmed, large-headed standard roses are both stylish and elegant. If properly trained and maintained, a standard rose can have a life span the same as any normal bush rose. So what is a standard exactly? Hybrid tea or floribunda rose cultivars can be budded at the top of rose stems (which are usually *Rosa rugosa* or *R. laxa*) some 1.2m (4ft) in height, instead of at ground level. It is this bare length of stem which provides extra height and which is so desirable in flowerbeds and borders where an extra dimension and focal point are required.

Whereas a bush rose may be pruned back to four or five buds from the base, a standard is pruned much less severely, perhaps to seven or eight buds from the graft union.

In most other respects standards are pruned just like hybrid teas, even down to the removal of suckers.

Keep the main stem free of any side growths – or feathers – by rubbing off any shoots as soon as they are seen.

Pruning a standard rose should be undertaken with a delicate touch and careful counting of the buds

Weeping standards

Weeping standards are usually taller than normal rose standards, even having as much as 2m (6ft) of bare stem. Rambler rose scions are grafted onto the stems, but the long flexible growth habit results in an attractive weeping feature.

In late summer, prune by removing all the shoots that have flowered during the past season. This will leave the younger growth, which will carry next year's flowers. It is important to keep the centre fairly open, so always prune to an outward facing bud.

If necessary, use wire training frames to keep the head of the plant under control; tying in stray shoots is better than cutting them out and losing the flowering potential of the plant.

Ground cover roses

These sorts of roses, either creeping ramblers or the slightly more upright modern shrub types, need very little pruning.

• cut out any dead or diseased stems
• tip prune the main stems
• shorten any laterals if they extend over their intended boundary.

With the rambler types, the stems will often root where they touch the ground (in the style of brambles, the closely related pernicious 'weed'). This can be a convenient way to, for example, cover a bank. But ensure you keep the plant under control – otherwise you will have a jungle of growth to eradicate.

Hedges & Topiary

Hedges are grown for a number of reasons and for a variety of effects. As a garden boundary, for example, a neat, close-growing hedge is very desirable. For privacy and security you may opt for a hedge with spikes and prickles to deter intruders. If there is a need to shelter a particular part of the garden from the prevailing winds, consider the tougher plants for hedging that can withstand being knocked around. If colour and flowers are more desirable than a straightforward 'formal' evergreen hedge, you will be better off with an informal hedge with long arching stems bearing flowers and leaves, stretching out and away from the base of the plant.

One step beyond trimming a hedge to a formal shape is the art of topiary. It is an ancient hobby; indeed, the Latin *toparius* means 'garden designer'. Topiary is the art of training and trimming trees and shrubs to clearly defined three-dimensional shapes. These are most commonly seen as birds, animals and, increasingly, pieces of furniture. Geometric shapes such as cones, archways, globes and spirals are common, too. Both broad-leaved and coniferous plants can be used. Not every gardener will

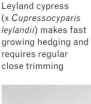

Leyland cypress (x *Cupressocyparis leylandii*) makes fast growing hedging and requires regular close trimming

Basic trimming

Hedge shrubs with small leaves, such as hawthorn (*Crataegus monogyna*), privet (*Ligustrum ovalifolium*) and yew (*Taxus baccata*) are best trimmed with shears, or one of the many makes of electric trimmer that are available. The latter saves an enormous amount of work if you have long lengths of vigorous hedging to tackle. With a short stretch of hedge, say around 1.8m (6ft) or so in length, a better result can be had with a sharp pair of shears. However, larger leaved shrubs such as laurel (*Prunus laurocerasus*) and conifers with arching branches (such as a loose-growing cypress), should only really be dealt with by a pair of secateurs.

> **TIP**
>
> To make a good formal hedge the plants should be well branched at the outset, and planted into well-prepared soil fairly closely. If the hedge is to be flat-topped or wide, it is a good idea to plant a double row.

want to indulge in topiary, but those who do, will need to know how and when to prune!

Formal Hedges

There are essentially two different hedge styles: formal and informal. The first is when a hedge has a tight-clipped surface, preferably down to soil level. Many conifers are used for formal hedging, and they do make ideal screens. The usual garden types include yew, Lawson's cypress (*Chamaecyparis lawsoniana*), Monterey cypress (*Cupressus macrocarpa*), Western red cedar (*Thuja occidentalis*) and the Leyland cypress (x *Cupressocyparis leylandii*). The latter has the distinction of being the fastest growing garden conifer. The adventurous gardener could try his hand

Correct hedge shapes

The drawings here show two right ways to train a formal hedge, and two wrong ways.

The sides of a formal hedge should slope outwards from the top to the base; this allows sunlight to reach the lower branches.

It is inadvisable to have straight sides, or sides which taper to the base. Here the upper branches will overshadow the lower ones, depriving them of light, which will result in bare, straggly shoots.

Also, with wide tops there is a risk during heavy snowfall that the upper, outer branches will be weighed down and will bend or snap. At best the hedge will look untidy, and at worst the plants will be damaged

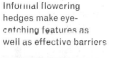

Avoid pruning in such a way that the top of the hedge becomes too wide

at planting and training hedges of some of the more compact pines, firs and spruces.

Informal Hedges

The informal hedge can be sub-divided into flowering, foliage and mixed hedging. With the last category, anything goes; you could have plants with good flowering potential (and later perhaps, autumn or winter berries), as well as plants grown for their coloured leaves. You could even opt for a few deciduous plants to give the hedge real character.

Flowering plants for informal hedges include golden bells (Forsythia), Japanese quince (Chaenomeles), flowering currants (Ribes) and sloe (*Prunus spinosa*). However, leaves can obscure flowers growing within the hedge, so it is important that each year you thin out some of the flowered growth. Leave at least two thirds of the branches intact, so that you are not depleting the density of the hedge too much and ruining the way it looks.

Informal flowering hedges make eye-catching features as well as effective barriers

Initial Training

The training of a hedge should be undertaken in the early stages of its life. You can't teach an old dog new tricks, nor can you successfully train old, established plants into an immaculately trimmed, impenetrable hedge. Indeed, in the first few years of any hedge, secateurs are the best tools to use for trimming, but once a formal outline and straight edges have been achieved, shears and mechanical trimmers come into their own.

It is most important to prune newly planted hedging plants to ensure that they do not grow too tall too quickly. This initial training should encourage the base of the plants to make plenty of growth.

Basic trimming

With practice, a gardener will develop a good eye and may well be able to trim a straight hedge without any aids. For the less experienced, a thin plank of wood can be used for guidance. Its length should be roughly the same as the height of the hedge. Lay the wood against the side of the hedge as you are trimming; you will be able to see easily which stems are protruding. Move the piece of wood as you work along.

Another method is to drive two stakes of equal height into the hedge and stretch a line tightly between the two (1). Make sure there is no sag in the line, otherwise the top will not be even (2).

1

2

Broadleaved hedges

In the case of upright, broadleaved plants such as privet (Ligustrum), hawthorn (Crataegus) and snowberry (*Symphoricarpos albus*), hard prune straight after planting. To encourage strong shoots from the base, cut back each plant to about 15cm (6in) from ground level. If you leave the plants unpruned at this time you run the risk of having plenty of top growth and bare bases.

During the following summer, lightly trim back the laterals to develop a bushier habit. During the second winter, cut back the new wood by about a half. Then trim the side shoots to within a 2–3cm (¾–1¼in) or so of the older framework. Again, the following summer, all you will need to do is trim back the tips.

Conifers

The story is different for conifers: at planting time the side shoots should be tipped back, and made less straggly. Do not hard prune the leaders, as with the

You can trim conifers with hedge trimmers, but if you cut back beyond green growth it will not return

deciduous shrubs; in fact, they need not be touched until the plants have reached the desired height. The following summer trim back the new growths to the required shape, and tie in the leaders to stakes as they grow. An established conifer hedge should need trimming only once during summer, to keep a desirable shape.

Hedge Problems

If a hedge develops bare patches at the base, or is allowed to become overgrown with long, straggly branches, you will need to take drastic action to restore it to good condition. Some species – including most conifers – will not tolerate this treatment, so will have to be replaced. Other plants might grow so slowly that it would be better to start afresh with new plants. On the other hand, it may be possible to disguise the problem by planting some strategically placed shrubs or climbers.

Renovation pruning

If you decide to do some severe pruning, then you should renovate each side of the hedge in different years, to avoid causing the plants too much stress. If there is to be a major reduction in height this, too, should be done separately, perhaps during a third year. In the case of deciduous shrubs, winter is generally the best time for renovation pruning, allowing a minimum amount of time before new growth starts, and therefore minimizing the duration of the ugly 'mutilated' condition. Evergreen shrubs should be tackled in mid-spring.

Cut back the branches, however long they have become, so that the cuts are around 15cm (6in) closer to the ground than the desired final size. There will be many dormant or hidden buds on the remaining stems and, all being well, these will be stimulated into growth. The resulting bushy growth can be clipped lightly for two to three years to form a dense surface, gradually thickening the hedge until it reaches the required size. Provided that you feed and mulch the hedge, and water it well during dry periods in summer, re-growth should be sufficiently rapid to hide the ugly, bare areas and exposed wounds within one or two years.

Replacing a hedge

If the species is unsuitable for hard pruning, you may feel that the most desirable option is to dig out the hedge completely, and then to replant the area with something new. However, this may be a very difficult task, particularly if the hedge is old or long, or access is difficult; the decision should not be undertaken lightly. The possibility of filling in bare bases, or covering up bare patches with new plants should not be overlooked. Either fill gaps with plants of the same species, or you could take the opportunity to introduce a new variety or two.

Concealing

Alternatively a low hedge or row of ornamentals could be grown at the hedge base to screen the bare areas. Suitable shade-tolerant plants for growing as a low hedge would include box (Buxus), shrubby honeysuckle (Lonicera) or Euonymus. To make an ornamental foreground you could grow lady's mantle (*Alchemilla mollis*), rose of Sharon (*Hypericum calycinum*) or ivy (Hedera).

Bare patches in coniferous hedges can be an unsightly problem, but judicious pruning will often help salvage the situation

Topiary

The art of topiary creates strong feelings varying from those who abhor it, to the other extreme, in which people consider it the ultimate in gardening skill. If you fancy trying it for yourself, however, remember that it is a hobby where results are looked for in decades rather than years...

Although box (Buxus) and yew (Taxus) are the most commonly seen plants used for topiary, there are many other trees and shrubs that are suitable: bay (*Laurus nobilis*), myrtle (*Myrtus communis*), *Lonicera nitida*, *Phillyrea angustifolia*, the Monterey cypress (*Cupressus macrocarpa*), the Italian cypress (*C. sempervirens*), holly (Ilex) and the Western red cedar (Thuja) are some of the best.

This basic peacock shape is traditionally popular and relatively easy to effect

Utility objects, such as furniture, bicycles, aeroplanes and the like are rather more challenging, as are animals and birds, which soon became popular once the early exponents of topiary first veered away from creating simple geometric shapes. The peacock is, perhaps, the epitome of

Box can easily be clipped into simple dome or ball shapes like this example

Geometric shapes and animals

The shape you choose to create is a matter of personal choice, but those of geometric form have always been popular: cubes, pyramids, domes, spirals, spheres and cones are frequently attempted, and modifications of these, such as the 'interrupted cone' which has a cake-stand like appearance. Round or square pillars can be most attractive, as well as archways (which are modified pillars).

You will need more advanced skills to attempt a shape like this stylized teapot

This set of 'garden furniture' will have taken a long period of careful training and cutting to bring to fruition

animalistic topiary, becoming very popular in the 19th and 20th centuries.

Training

It is best to start from scratch, by planting a young tree or shrub in spring; the first trimming will take place in summer. In the first year, do not remove the growing points; instead, cut the side shoots hard to encourage the development of a well-furnished base. After the first couple of years, trim more lightly, aiming to produce the shape required.

Cubes, pillars and archways will have vertical sides, but in all other forms sides will be tapering. To create the shapes you will almost certainly need to use some aids, from stakes and wires to metal hoops. Shoots will need to be tied in to these so that, as the young wood ripens, it remains in shape.

There is not the room here to show how to create different topiary shapes, but there are many excellent books on the subject that take the reader through every stage of the creation, including the more intricate shapes.

Routine maintenance

Once the framework of any figure has been established, its outline must be kept sharp by regular trimming. Unlike most other forms of pruning, this is not particularly seasonal. You should, of course, give the plants a good 'haircut' at least once a year, the timing to suit both you and the plant. To keep the figure looking good, remove any vigorous or protruding shoots whenever they are seen.

For curved surfaces and intricate figures it is best to use a pair of sharp shears. A powered hedge cutter can be used for simple geometric shapes.

Trimming topiary with hand shears should be carried out regularly to keep a defined shape

Ornamental Woody Plants

The following ornamental woody plant directory offers practical information on pruning and training the trees, shrubs and climbing plants most commonly found in our gardens.

Choisya ternata

Acer palmatum

There is one sentence you will not see too often in this directory section, yet it is vitally important for the welfare of woody plants: when pruning, always cut out dead, diseased or damaged wood, when seen. This applies to every type of woody plant, regardless of the normal pruning season. If you leave unpruned any dead or diseased wood, healthy tissue will become infected; likewise, if a branch is damaged, then there are multiple entry points for air- and water-borne infections. So, even though this sentence is not repeated hundreds of times throughout the text, you should be aware that it applies to every plant entry appearing on the following pages.

Abies   Fir

EVERGREEN CONIFER

General: These conifers do not pose any significant pruning challenges for the gardener. From the moment a seedling of Abies is manageable, it is important that a single leader is selected. Once planted in its permanent quarters you should allow the leader, and all side branches, to grow unchecked. Any branches which are seen to be damaged, or are dying back, should be removed to the trunk. No other pruning is normally necessary.

Abutilon

EVERGREEN/DECIDUOUS SHRUB

General: All species are tender, and if grown outdoors are best protected by a south-facing wall. Although these are short-lived plants, often exhausting themselves in three or four years, they do repay by flowering over a long period in summer. They flower on current season's growth. Before growth starts in earnest in mid-spring, cut out any winter damage, and thin out crowded shoots.
Special requirements: *Abutilon* x *suntense* is a spectacular hardy hybrid which tends to blow over

Abies koreana

unless it is fairly hard pruned after flowering, in late spring or early summer.

A. vitifolium should be treated as a freestanding shrub; the only pruning needed is dead-heading, in mid-summer.

The trailing abutilon, A. megapotamicum, grows long, slender stems, and it is ideal for training against a wall. The form 'Variegatum' has yellow-mottled leaves. With a wall-trained specimen, cut away old wood in early to mid-spring, and tie in the strong young replacement shoots.

Acacia   Silver wattle
EVERGREEN SHRUB/TREE

General: Native of Australasia, acacias succeed only in mild districts, and are best grown in the shelter of a warm wall. The only pruning required to keep a mature specimen producing its masses of tiny yellow blooms each spring is to remove old, spent flower shoots, dead wood (of which there tends to be a large amount each year), and any frost-damaged tips. This is best carried out soon after flowering is over, during mid- to late spring, and ideally when you know there are no more prolonged frosts until autumn.
Special requirements: Most acacias resent hard pruning, and do not regenerate successfully. However two exceptions to this are Acacia dealbata and A. melanoxylon; both are suckering species. Vigorous species (such as A. dealbata and A. longifolia) can be cut back hard when young to encourage branching low down. Some forms, including A. cultiformis and A. verticillata can be clipped regularly, and make acceptable informal hedging.

Acer   Maple
DECIDUOUS SHRUB/TREE

General: There are a large number of acers, varying in height, habit and decorative value. It is the smaller Japanese maple (Acer palmatum) which is most commonly seen in gardens. These acers tend to branch low; if they do not, a little judicious pruning whilst they are young will encourage them.

There are dozens of Acer species that make wonderful specimen trees. Many are grown for their ornamental barks, whilst others have desirable shapes and leaf styles and colours.

All acers, however, appreciate an acid soil, and should be allowed to grow at will, removing only unwanted branches in winter (not any other time as maples can 'bleed' sap). Dead wood can be removed in summer, and small cuts to remove reverted shoots on variegated plants whilst in leaf, can be made in late summer or early autumn.
Special requirements: The Norway maple (Acer platanoides) produces a tight head with heavy branching. There is often a mass of dwarf shoots growing along the length of the framework, and gardeners are often tempted to remove these, or to thin the tree out. Do not, for this is the normal habit of the tree.

The common or field maple (A. campestre), the Japanese maple (A. palmatum) and the full-moon maple (A. japonicum) should be treated the same. Only remove badly placed or crossing shoots. Keep pruning of established plants to a minimum. With A. palmatum it is important to keep neighbouring trees and shrubs pruned back, in order to encourage the free branching nature of this species. Its stems can be inhibited if they come into contact with nearby plants.

Acers grown for their attractive barks include the snakebark maples (A. davidii and A. pensylvanicum) and the paperbark maple (A. griseum). In order to appreciate the feature of the bark, the aim with these trees should be to train as straight, and as clearly visible a trunk as possible. As the trees grow, clear the trunks of side shoots and low branches, up to at least 1.5m (5ft) from the ground. Similarly, as the crown of the tree develops, cut out twiggy or crossing branches that will obscure the bark higher up.

Actinidia
DECIDUOUS CLIMBER

General: This genus also gives us the Kiwi fruit, *see page 134*. All actinidias are vigorous climbers. The most often seen form is *Actinidia kolomikta*, with its attractive green leaves, many of which are half coloured bright pink. It is slightly tender, and needs plenty of space to grow.
Special requirements: Once a well-spaced framework has been achieved, cut back young stems in mid-spring to two or three buds of the older wood. If you do not carry out this annual maintenance pruning the plant will still show off its leaves, but may soon outgrow its space.

Aesculus   Horse chestnut, or Buckeye
DECIDUOUS TREE

General: These make superb specimen trees in large gardens, and there are a few smaller forms. The most common form is the true horse chestnut (*Aesculus hippocastanum*), which produces large candles of white, pink or red flowers in mid- to late spring. These come from buds on wood produced the previous year.
Special requirements: Trees may be slow to establish. At the start select a leader with well-spaced laterals. Occasionally young leaders may be lost through frost or drying winds, so retrain a new leader, otherwise two will result because the tree produces opposite buds. *A. parviflora*, which is valuable for its late summer flowers, does not form a tree but clumps of vertical shoots. Occasionally remove the oldest of these and restrict the spread, otherwise the clump may become invasive. This should be carried out during winter.

Ailanthus   Tree of Heaven
DECIDUOUS TREE

General: *Ailanthus altissima*, originally from China, is valued for its compound ash-like leaves, which emerge in spring bright red, later turning to green. It is too big to grow in a small garden, as it achieves an eventual height of some 20m (65ft).
Special requirements: The only way to make Ailanthus suitable for a smaller garden is to cut all shoots back to pollard in spring, followed by an application of general fertiliser to encourage regrowth. Take care not to damage the roots at all, as extensive suckering will result.

Alnus   Alder
DECIDUOUS SHRUB/TREE

General: Plants for damp, moist soils, perfect against a pond or lake. They are grown especially for their decorative catkins in winter and spring. Often they are allowed to develop without special training, except for thinning out crowded branches. The common alder (*Alnus glutinosa*) is plain green, but *A. glutinosa* 'Aurea' has leaves of pale yellow.
Special requirements: If a tree is required, rather than a shrub, select a central leader and well-spaced laterals. Coloured leaf forms should be hard pruned after flowering. The grey alder (*A. incana*) will sucker, and these can be separated to propagate the tree.

Amelanchier   Snowy mespilus
DECIDUOUS SHRUB/TREE

General: These are beautiful, very hardy plants which produce abundant white flowers in spring, blackish fruits in summer and autumn, and some of the best autumn leaf tints. One of the smaller forms, and therefore better for the garden perhaps, is *A. canadensis*.
Special requirements: You may allow your plant to sucker heavily and remain a shrub, in which case it should be pruned in mid-winter when the oldest stems are removed. Alternatively you can make the plant more like a single-stemmed tree; a central leader is trained, and all side shoots are retained for as long as possible, but reduced when necessary. Prune during the dormant season.

Amelanchier canadensis

Ampelopsis   Blueberry climber
DECIDUOUS CLIMBER

General: A good garden climber, for covering a fence or house wall, it will thrive in either sun or shade. All forms are strong growers that support themselves by tendrils and need plenty of space. It also needs good support, aided by ties and wires, as it will not always cling to smooth walls. They are well suited for growing through a tree where no pruning is required. Noted for its red leaf tints in autumn and dark blue fruits (hence its common name), several members of the genus are now classified under Parthenocissus, *see page 82*.
Special requirements: If space is restricted, train in a number of shoots and in mid-winter cut back all young shoots to within two or three buds of the main stems. Stems will 'bleed' if pruning is carried out after the sap begins to rise in spring.

Aesculus indica

Aralia
Devil's walking stick, or Japanese angelica tree

DECIDUOUS SHRUB

General: The chief attraction is the large compound leaves of which there are variegated forms. Aralia gets its common name from the suckers which appear as stout rods, or 'walking sticks'. Watch out for the sharp spines!

Special requirements: Stems arising from a rootstock are stout and pithy, and liable to be damaged in winter if they do not ripen properly. Retain only a few stems and remove the rest at ground level each spring. If you desire bigger, bolder foliage coppice in spring.

Araucaria araucana
Monkey puzzle

EVERGREEN CONIFER

General: The common name arises from the very sharp foliage that makes climbing difficult. It makes a large tree and requires plenty of space.

Special requirements: Initially, select a central leader with well-spaced side branches. Retain these until they die naturally, then cut them off at the base. No regular pruning required.

Arbutus
Strawberry tree

EVERGREEN SHRUB/TREE

General: *Arbutus menziesii*, *A. andrachne* and *A. x andrachnoides* have attractive barks, whilst *A. unedo* is the best form for flowers and fruits. Shrubs require little attention except to thin growths in mid-spring. Trees should have a central leader with all side shoots reduced. Straggly old specimens will regenerate if cut back hard in late winter.

Special requirements: Whereas most Arbutus can be grown as either trees or shrubs, *A. menziesii* should, if at all possible, be grown with a single main trunk; this better suits the later habit of the tree.

Arbutus unedo

Aucuba japonica 'Variegata'

Aristolochia
Dutchman's pipe

DECIDUOUS CLIMBER

General: These are vigorous climbers needing plenty of space. The pipe-shaped blooms are yellowish brown, and are often obscured by the heart-shaped leaves.

Special requirements: After flowering, drastically thin out shoots, and cut back any that are wandering.

Artemisia
Wormwood

EVERGREEN SHRUB/PERENNIAL

General: Plants of this genus are mainly grown in gardens for their scented grey foliage; the flowers are insignificant. Cut back herbaceous perennials in mid- to late autumn. Remove winter damage to shrubby forms in mid-spring and trim to shape. As these plants are grown for their foliage, flower spikes can be removed as they form.

Special requirements: Cut the common wormwood (*Artemisia absinthium*) back to 15cm (6in) high in mid-spring.

Aucuba
Spotted laurel

EVERGREEN SHRUB/PERENNIAL

General: *Aucuba japonica* is a useful hardy and shade-tolerant shrub with a bushy habit and large, deep green and waxy leaves. Trim to shape in mid-spring, occasionally cutting out some of the oldest wood. This shrub will respond to hard pruning if it becomes too large.

Special requirements: The sexes are on different plants, and it is only the females that produce the bright red berries. However you will need to plant both sexes if berries are to be produced. All-green shoots may grow on a variegated form – remove these as soon as they are seen.

Berberis — Barberry

DECIDUOUS/EVERGREEN SHRUB

General: All evergreen berberis species should be pruned after flowering, but if you want them to display their attractive berries delay pruning until late spring. At this time remove the shoots that have carried the fruits. Most deciduous forms, including the popular *Berberis thunbergii*, develop dense thickets and these should be thinned in mid-summer, removing completely any overcrowded branches, even down to ground level if needed.

Special requirements: If old bushes become unmanageable, they can be cut down to ground level after flowering, for they will readily re-grow. *Berberis x ottawensis* 'Superba' is a particularly vigorous form, and requires hard pruning every year; this also encourages the production of the attractive young red stems and bronzy leaves.

Betula — Birch

DECIDUOUS TREE

General: Any pruning should be carried out when the trees are dormant; bleeding of sap will occur at other times. When training, select a central leader and well-spaced laterals, exposing the trunk eventually to about 3m (10ft) before allowing the branches to form. The leader in birches is often lost, and potential replacement leaders may be in competition with each other so you should pick the strongest or best placed. Weeping birches should have a central leading shoot (not a 'leader' in the normal sense, as these are weeping trees) trained to a support until there is a clear stem of 3m (10ft) or more.

Special requirements: *Betula pendula* 'Youngii' has a naturally weeping habit and, if left to its own devices, may become broader than its height. You can, however, encourage 'vertical' growth: in the early years take the flexible leading shoot, and train it to a vertical stake, perhaps up to 4m (12ft). Also, remove any shoots below the graft union, which is probably some 2m (6ft) up the tree.

Buddleja — Butterfly bush

DECIDUOUS/EVERGREEN SHRUB

General: *Buddleja davidii* is the familiar shrub which flowers in mid-summer on new wood, so should be pruned in late winter; it can be pruned hard, back to

Buddleja davidii

some 45cm (18in) from the ground.

Special requirements: The orange ball tree (*Buddleja globosa*) produces globular, orange blooms, and can become bare at the base, so is perhaps best grown at the rear of a flower border. *B. alternifolia* is best treated as a standard. Select the strongest shoot, removing the others, and tie to a stake; retain a clear stem of 1.2m (4ft), after which the natural development of the plant can be allowed. This form blooms on the previous year's wood, so prune it in mid-summer, after flowering.

Buxus — Box

EVERGREEN SHRUB/TREE

General: The common box (*Buxus sempervirens*) is an excellent plant for use as a small, formal hedge, also ideal for topiary. If you choose to grow it in tree form, select a single leader, cutting out any competitors. Side shoots should be reduced and thinned if necessary. If growing it as a shrub, trim it to shape in mid-spring.

Special requirements: If winter snow has damaged some of the shoots by weighing them down, corrective pruning may be necessary. *Buxus balearica* is a larger form, with a more open habit; prune it regularly to keep it compact. It may also be damaged by severe frosts.

Buxus sempervirens

Callicarpa

DECIDUOUS SHRUB

General: These medium-sized shrubs are grown for their clusters of bright purple bead-like berries, carried throughout autumn and winter. Both the usual form, *Callicarpa bodinieri* var. *giraldii*, and the less common *C. rubella*, should be treated the same. Both are tender to some degree. Prune in spring, after heavy frosts have passed, and before new growth gets away. Remove any winter damage and thin out crowded shoots.

Special requirements: Callicarpas that may appear to have been killed by the winter cold may re-grow if you remove the dead shoots, back to ground level if necessary. Do this in early spring.

Callistemon — Bottle brush

EVERGREEN SHRUB

General: Growth is continuous, the red or yellow flowers being produced in summer, just behind the growing point. Seed capsules can remain on the shrub for years but, if left, these gradually reduce the rate of growth producing a gaunt, rather untidy bush. Prune them after flowering, removing the spent flowers, and trim to shape.

Special requirements: Tip-prune young plants to encourage a bushy shape.

Calluna   Ling
EVERGREEN SHRUB

General: All cultivars of *Calluna vulgaris* should be grown in the same way. Trim over the clumps in late winter or early spring, removing old flowers and most of the previous year's growth. Plants that are grown just for foliage are often best trimmed just before the flower spikes develop, because the colours of foliage and flower often clash.

Special requirements: Dwarf forms such as 'Foxii' and 'Foxii Nana' are not pruned at all, except to remove dead wood or the occasional over-long shoot.

Calluna vulgaris 'Silver Knight'

Camellia
EVERGREEN SHRUB

General: Grow the slightly tender species as free-standing plants under the shelter of a wall, or fan-train a well-spaced framework and allow side branches to develop just sufficiently to fill the intervening spaces; remove surplus shoots as well as any coming away from the wall. *Camellia japonica* and its many forms are hardier. Deadhead those kinds that do not shed their spent flowers naturally; at the same time trim to shape or to restrict growth.

Special requirements: With *C. japonica* several colours can appear amongst flowers on one bush. Trace branches bearing different coloured flowers back to their source and remove. Species that flower in the autumn, such as *C. sasanqua*, should only be pruned, if necessary, during mid-spring.

Campsis   Trumpet vine
DECIDUOUS CLIMBER

General: *Campsis grandiflora* is a slightly tender climber that does best on a sunny wall. It produces deep orange trumpet-shaped flowers during late summer and autumn, on current year's wood. It is a strong grower, attaching itself to supports by small aerial stem roots. Sometimes it will require tying in to wires or eye-bolts in a solid wall. Once a well-shaped framework has been trained with the lower part of the wall well clothed, all side shoots should be cut back in late winter or early spring to within two or three buds of the older wood.

Special requirements: *Campsis radicans* produces a greater quantity of stem roots, and is therefore completely self-clinging when established.

Carpinus   Hornbeam
DECIDUOUS TREE

General: A hardy tree with spring catkins, corrugated leaves in summer, golden leaf tints and winged fruits in autumn and grey bark in winter. In a garden situation you are most likely to see hornbeam grown as a formal hedge (it is also suitable for pleaching). In the case of a standard tree, train to a single leader with well-spaced laterals. Carry out pruning from late summer to mid-winter, for if delayed until the sap starts to rise in spring, bleeding will follow.

Special requirements: Coral spot disease can be troublesome both on dead and living wood, so cut this away as soon as it is seen.

Camellia japonica 'Lavinia Maggi'

Caryopteris   Blue spiraea
DECIDUOUS SHRUB

General: *Caryopteris* x *clandonensis* and its various cultivars produce blue flowers in early autumn. The plant forms into a rounded mound, which looks attractive tumbling over a low wall. Unless the wood is thoroughly ripened, dieback is common. In mid-spring cut back all young shoots to some 5cm (2in) of the framework, which is best trained on a short leg.

Special requirements: *Caryopteris incana* is slightly taller and requires less maintenance pruning; just cut back any dead shoot tips as the buds are breaking in spring.

Castanea
Sweet chestnut

see page 122

Catalpa
Indian bean tree

DECIDUOUS SHRUB/TREE

General: Genus of small or medium-sized trees with magnificent foliage and summer flowers, followed in autumn and winter by seedpods, which eventually turn black. Often trained as a large shrub with several leaders. If grown in this way, keep the centre of the bush open. If grown as a tree, train to a single leader, with well spaced side branches. Pruning, when necessary, is carried out during early to mid-spring, when the old seedpods are removed. Older specimens need regular removal of dead wood. All pruning should be carried out in winter, when the plant is dormant.

Special requirements: When grown for their coloured foliage, such as the golden-leaved *Catalpa bignonioides* 'Aurea', pruning should be moderately hard. Catalpas may be pollarded, which results in an increase in size of the leaves.

Catalpa erubescens 'Purpurea'

Ceanothus
Californian lilac

DECIDUOUS/EVERGREEN SHRUB

General: Produces clusters of flowers in various shades of blue, from mid-spring to early autumn depending on variety. The evergreen forms are tender, and often seen grown against a wall. Prune after flowering, cutting only the young growth hard back to the framework. If treated as free-standing shrubs, train to several leaders and trim each year, following flowering, back to this framework; winter damage should be removed and some thinning may be desirable. The deciduous kinds flower on current season's growth, which is cut down to ground level, or to a framework, in mid-spring.

Special requirements: With the evergreen forms, avoid cutting into old wood, as this is slow to break.

Ceanothus 'Cascade'

Cedrus atlantica (male cones)

Cedrus
Cedar

EVERGREEN CONIFER

General: Young cedars are triangular in outline but with age all develop flat tops. Select and retain a central leader, removing any competition, multiple leaders, or strong growth that develops from low down. Whenever you take the saw or loppers to a cedar make sure you always leave some live foliage on the branch, otherwise it will die.

Special requirements: *Cedrus deodara* is the most suitable cedar for a small garden; it produces a pendulous leading shoot, known as a 'dropper'. Do not prune this, as it will suppress the development of the tree.

Celastrus
Bittersweet or Staff vine

DECIDUOUS CLIMBER

General: *Celastrus orbiculatus* is a strong climber best suited to growing over a tree, wall or trellis where it can be left to its own devices. If space is restricted, annual thinning is necessary to keep it within bounds; this is best carried out in mid-summer when it is easier to recognize dead wood. Cut out a few of the oldest stems each year, and aim to keep the centre of the plant open.

Special requirements: *Celastrus scandens* is a stronger vine, and it is best grown through a sturdy tree, rather than a fence or piece of trelliswork.

Ceratostigma

EVERGREEN SHRUB

General: The tender *Ceratostigma willmottianum* bears brilliant blue flowers on current season's wood from mid-summer to early autumn. Although it may be cut back to ground level in a cold winter, it usually breaks

C. willmottianum

away freely so long as the roots are undamaged. All growth surviving the winter is cut back to ground level in mid-spring.

Special requirements: There is a herbaceous perennial *C. plumbaginoides*; clear away old growth in the spring, just as the new shoots are emerging.

Cercis   Judas tree
DECIDUOUS TREE

General: Cercis is generally grown as a multi-stemmed shrub, with little pruning. It is important to train in a satisfactory framework, and this will need a light annual trim in the formative years. Do this after flowering, and at the same time remove the immature seed pods. The production of these can be excessive and if left will reduce the vigour and extension growth.

Special requirements: *Cercis canadensis* 'Forest Pansy' is an extremely popular form, with deep reddish purple leaves and pink flowers in spring. This form is generally grown on a single, clear stem up to some 1m (3ft) before the branches are allowed to radiate outwards.

Chaenomeles   Ornamental quince or
                                               Japanese quince
DECIDUOUS SHRUB

General: Late winter and spring flowering shrubs, which in hot summers set aromatic, yellow-green fruits. Chaenomeles is a spur-bearing shrub, and once regular flowering begins, little pruning is required. Select several leaders and train to a well-branched framework. It is important to keep the centre of the bush open and any shoots intruding should be removed.

Special requirements: If grown as a wall shrub it should be trained as a fan. All side shoots are then shortened, and after the spur system has formed no further pruning should be required. To encourage spur production in the early years, cut back all side shoots to three or four buds in the winter months.

Cercis siliquastrum

Chamaecyparis   False cypress
EVERGREEN CONIFER

General: Grown for their shape and long-lasting evergreen foliage. Do not prune to shape, as you will expose much older wood, which will not regenerate readily. The main species found in gardens is the Lawson cypress (*Chamaecyparis lawsoniana*), which makes excellent hedges. Like most hedging conifers, it can only be clipped into live foliage. Unpruned trees can also be used for tall screens and windbreaks. The dwarf and small-growing kinds need no pruning.

Special requirements: Many Chamaecyparis naturally produce several leaders. In their early years these are no trouble, but with age the leaders are likely to fall away and spoil the outline; surreptitious wiring then becomes necessary to pull them together.

Chimonanthus   Winter sweet
DECIDUOUS SHRUB

General: *Chimonanthus praecox* produces beautifully scented waxy blooms throughout winter, but does not flower freely unless the wood is properly ripened. For this reason it is often grown against a wall. In mid-summer, cut back all side branches to two or three buds of the main framework. For free-standing shrubs, allow several leaders to be trained; every year in mid-summer all side shoots should be shortened back to two or three buds.

Special requirements: If the early part of the summer is particularly wet, before the end of the season you should thin out any excess growth to encourage better ripening.

Choisya   Mexican orange blossom
EVERGREEN SHRUB

General: Normally fast growing, choisyas naturally develop into well-shaped flowering shrubs without any pruning. *Choisya ternata* is the most widely seen form; *Choisya* 'Aztec Pearl' has narrower, elongated leaves. Both forms may be damaged in a cold winter, so plant them in a position protected from cold winds.

Special requirements: Remove the flower heads when they fade (they can bloom sporadically throughout the whole year). Trim them to shape, if required, at the same time.

Cistus   Sun rose or Rock rose
EVERGREEN SHRUB

General: Generally produce an abundance of short-lived flowers during late spring and early summer, their rounded bushes covered by large, flat blooms. All species are tender to some extent. Following flowering, remove dead flowers and their stems as well as any winter damage, and trim to shape.

Special requirements: Young plants may be pruned to encourage bushiness, but remember that old plants do not respond well to being cut back hard, and so it is better to replace them.

Chamaecyparis lawsoniana 'Gimbornii'

Cistus 'Silver Pink'

Clematis

DECIDUOUS/EVERGREEN CLIMBER

If left unpruned, most Clematis develop into tangled masses of growth, bearing their flowers high up above leafless, woody stems. The aim with all of the following techniques is to provide the maximum coverage and flower in the space available, and at a reasonable height. There are three basic rules, based on the age of the wood on which the flower buds develop.

Pruning at planting time

Many forms of Clematis, particularly the larger-flowered hybrids, will tend to grow rapidly upwards on a single stem during the first season after planting unless checked at an early stage.

At planting time, cut back the stem to the lowest pair of strong buds to encourage the plant to produce further basal growth. The two stems produced from these buds can be stopped again to increase the number of basal shoots, but this is usually unnecessary.

This initial pruning applies to all clematis, whether planted dormant in winter, or in leaf during spring or early summer.

Group 1 pruning

Group 1 consists mainly of vigorous species which flower from mid- to late spring on short shoots from growth produced the previous summer.

Initial pruning at planting will encourage vigorous growth that can be gently guided to cover the area available and to form the basic framework over a two-year period. Once this has been achieved the pruning of mature plants consists of cutting away all the flowered wood to within 5–8cm (2–3in) of the main framework immediately after flowering. This will stimulate new, long and vigorous growth that can be trained or tied in as required, or allowed to cascade naturally. This growth will provide next season's flowering display and must not be winter-pruned.

Examples of species in this group are *C. montana* and its forms, *C. cirrhosa*, *C. alpina* and

Clematis montana 'Grandiflora'

Clematis 'Nelly Moser'

C. macropetala. Be aware that attempting to restrict the first two in this list to limited areas on a wall or fence can result in a good deal of work; they are best given ample space on a house wall or in a tree. If left unpruned, or merely sheared over after flowering to keep them tidy, they may require rejuvenation after a few years. This involves cutting them to near ground level in winter.

Group 2 pruning

The second group contains all the hybrids that provide large, sumptuous flowers during late spring and early summer on the previous year's wood. While the flowers are being produced on side-shoots from the old wood, new growth is being formed. This produces further crops of medium-sized blooms during late summer and early autumn.

The growth habit of Group 2 clematis makes them difficult to prune satisfactorily without a good deal of work, and it is often thought best to leave them entirely unpruned, or only lightly pruned, until they become straggly and out of control. Then the rejuvenation process can be applied. Alternatively, they may be treated as Group 1 and pruned back hard to base each winter, but then they will only flower in late summer.

Clematis cirrhosa

Pruning *Clematis montana*

This is a vigorous species (Group 1), best grown on large walls, long fences or through trees. It can be left unpruned unless it gets too large or out of control. If this occurs it is possible to renovate the plant by cutting the old stems hard back in late winter or early spring, to within 60–100cm (2–3ft) of the ground. In most cases dormant buds on the remaining old, woody shoots are stimulated into growth, and within a year or two the plant should be flowering freely again. If the plant is particularly old, with a sizeable 'trunk' you may have to make the pruning height rather further up the plant. As with all renovation techniques, it is important to indulge the plants in a generous campaign of feeding and watering.

Popular cultivars in this group include 'Henryi', 'Nelly Moser', 'The President', 'Mme le Coultre', 'William Kennett', and the double flowered 'Duchess of Edinburgh' and 'Vyvyan Pennell'.

Group 3 pruning

The final group contains all the Clematis species and hybrids that flower in summer and autumn entirely on new growth produced during the current season. If left unpruned they begin growth in the spring from where they flowered the previous season and rapidly become bare at the base with flowers at the top only.

Pruning is very simple, consisting of cutting back the whole of the previous year's growth virtually to ground level in mid- to late winter. The pruning cuts should be made immediately above the lowest pair of strong buds on each stem.

Examples of Clematis in this group are *C. orientalis*, *C. tangutica*, *C. texensis* hybrids such as 'Gravetye Beauty' and 'Etoile Violette', *C. viticella* and its cultivars; and among the large flowered hybrids there are 'Ernest Markham', 'Hagley Hybrid', 'Perle d'Azur' and *C.* x *jackmanii*.

Clerodendrum

EVERGREEN/DECIDUOUS SHRUB/CLIMBER

General: All species are tender and frequently cut back in a cold winter, though they break away again readily from below ground level. *Clerodendrum bungei* (the glory flower) is an upright, evergreen shrub with fragrant pink flowers in late summer. Cut out any winter damage, and reduce the longest shoots in mid-spring. The same pruning regime applies to the deciduous *C. trichotomum*; this species has a tendency to sucker, particularly if the root system is damaged in any way.

Special requirements: The bleeding heart vine (*C. thomsoniae*) is a vigorous climber with white hanging flowers in summer. This can be tipped back at the same time as any deadheading, but it is better to replace an old plant rather than to prune it back hard.

Clerodendrum trichotomum

Clianthus   Lobster claw or Parrot's bill

EVERGREEN SHRUB

General: *Clianthus puniceus* is a sprawling tender shrub that needs the support and protection of a sunny wall. Striking salmon-pink flowers, in late spring and summer, are carried on wood produced in the previous year. Following blooming remove those shoots which have borne flowers. Seed set can be heavy and if these are left to ripen the vigour of the plant declines.

Special requirements: If you need to shorten healthy stems, in order to keep them within bounds, do not cut away more than a third or so of the length, as this will suppress further development of the plant.

Clematis 'Henryi'

Clianthus puniceus 'Cardinal'

Cornus   Cornel, Dogwood
DECIDUOUS SHRUB/TREE

General: The Cornus genus is a large one, comprising mainly deciduous trees and shrubs, although there are a few evergreens, and even one or two herbaceous forms. For pruning purposes this genus can be divided into those plants that sucker and those that develop a single stem.

Suckering Cornus
These tend to make clumps and should be thinned out during late winter when all shoots that have carried fruit can be removed. A number of these shrubs have attractively coloured stems, which are cut to ground level annually in early spring. Included within this group is *Cornus alba* and its cultivars: it has a spreading habit, forming a thicket of bright red stems, attractive in winter, but rather rampant. There is also *C. stolonifera* 'Flaviramea', with attractive greenish yellow winter bark.
Special requirements: Allow any Cornus grown for its winter stems to grow unpruned for the first year after planting, so as to become fully established in the ground, and to develop a good root system. Then, in early spring two years after planting, cut all stems back to two buds of the previous year's wood.

Single stem Cornus
The Cornelian cherry (*C. mas*) is a large shrub, or can be trained in to a small tree some 4.5m (125ft) high. It is arguably the best of the flowering dogwoods: tiny bright yellow flower clusters appear in mid- to late winter. *Cornus kousa* chinensis is a slightly smaller tree, with white bracts producing tiers of blooms in late spring. *Cornus florida rubra* produces smallish pink flowers in spring. With all of these species, the time for pruning – which should ideally be kept to a minimum – is early summer. Thin the branches, if necessary, to show off the flowers better.

Cornus 'Porlock'

Corylus   Hazel, Cobnuts and Filberts

see page 123

Cotinus   Smoke bush
EVERGREEN SHRUB

General: *Cotinus coggygria* is grown both for its smoky flowers and decorative leaves, and there is little pruning required except to thin out crowded shoots, and to tip shoots in the winter months.

When growing the purple-leaved forms, including the Purpureus Group, for autumn colour, where you require young fresh stems and foliage at the expense of flowers, then you should hard prune in the winter months.
Special requirements: *Cotinus obovatus* is similar in appearance, and is better suited to growing as a bush with many laterals and side shoots. Only remove overcrowded shoots, and shoot tips in the early years to encourage bushiness.

Cotinus coggygria 'Royal Purple'

Cotoneaster
EVERGREEN/DECIDUOUS SHRUB/TREE

General: The strongest growing kinds, such as *Cotoneaster frigida*, can be trained to a single leader with well-spaced laterals so as to form trees. Shrubby cotoneasters just require thinning and tipping back to keep them within bounds; evergreens are pruned in mid-spring and the deciduous kinds in winter. The prostrate forms, which are used as ground cover, benefit from an occasional thinning to let in the light. *C. horizontalis* lends itself to training against a wall that gets little or no direct sunlight. Form a well-spaced framework, removing any branches that come away from the wall.
Special requirements: There are one or two pendulous forms, such as *C. salicifolia*, which can be trained as weeping standards. A single leader is trained up a stake and all side shoots pinched back until there is a clear 2m (6ft) stem. Sometimes they are high grafted on to a 2m (6ft) stem. Cut back all side shoots in mid-spring and train in a well-spaced framework. Note that fireblight is a troublesome disease with this genus.

Crataegus   Thorn
DECIDUOUS SHRUB/TREE

General: In addition to the may, common names for members of the Crataegus genus include quickthorn and hawthorn, which suggests that they have dangerous spines which can attack anyone, but pruners in particular! Almost all species will form small trees if trained to a single leader; they are, being small in stature, well suited to training as standards. Following training, the only pruning

be retained for as long as possible.

Special requirements: *Cupressus sempervirens* is particularly susceptible to weather damage: high winds and even heavy snowfall on the branches can sometimes take their toll, which will necessitate reparative pruning.

Cytisus   Broom
DECIDUOUS SHRUB

General: All brooms flower profusely in spring and early summer. Prune them immediately after flowering, cutting back to where new shoots are breaking. Avoid cutting into old wood, as it is likely to cause dieback. At the same time cut out crowded shoots and open up the centre of the bush.

Special requirements: *Cytisus battandieri* (the pineapple broom) is slightly tender and often grown against a wall. Either as a wall shrub or free standing, it needs little pruning except for cutting out winter damage in mid-spring. Thin and cut out some of the old wood occasionally.

Daboecia   St Dabeoc's heath
EVERGREEN SHRUB

General: This is a small genus of dwarf evergreen shrubs, whose flowers resemble those of the bell heathers. Clip over the bushes in mid-spring, taking off the old flower stalks and most of the last year's growth. Trim to shape at the same time.

Special requirements: Straggly plants may be cut back harder, but only to about half-way along the stems.

Daphne
EVERGREEN/DECIDUOUS SHRUB

General: Daphnes are noted for their strongly fragrant flowers, which are also decorative, and which in the most popular species come during late winter. In general these shrubs are left unpruned. If the prostrate kinds, including *Daphne cneorum*, develop long, bare stems, these should be pegged down and covered with soil, they will root and, in time, form dense clumps.

Special requirements: *D. mezereum*, commonly called the mezereon, should be pruned, as without attention it becomes gaunt, with long bare stems. Each spring remove those twigs that have carried the flowers.

necessary, which should be carried out in winter, is to remove crossing branches and to thin out overcrowded branches. If you want to grow a shrubby form, train in three leaders. Later pruning consists of simply keeping the centre of the bush open and carrying out judicious thinning in early spring.

Special requirements: If grown as a hedge, one annual trim, in summer, is usually all that is necessary. Fireblight is a troublesome disease with this genus.

x Cupressocyparis   Leyland cypress
EVERGREEN CONIFER

General: x *Cupressocyparis leylandii* is probably the fastest growing hybrid conifer, various achieving 2m (6ft) of new growth each year. It makes a tall specimen tree on its own, but is perhaps more familiar as a hedging plant. Select and retain a single leader. Avoid trimming hedges in the spring when birds are nesting.

Special requirements: Golden-leaved Leyland cypress, which are less vigorous and so require less trimming, are now available.

Cupressus   Cypress
EVERGREEN CONIFER

General: This is a genus of soft conifers, not unlike the Leyland cypress, but much less vigorous. Select and retain a single leader, shortening back the side branches on the spreading species. In general no trimming is necessary and all side shoots should

Davidia involucrata var. vilmoriniana

Davidia
Handkerchief tree

DECIDUOUS TREE

General: A free-standing tree, the common name refers to the blooms that appear in mid-spring – two large, white bracts surrounding tiny flowers. Sometimes with young trees the leaves on the ends of the branches fall prematurely in autumn, making one believe that the shoot tips are dying. Do not worry, as this is an idiosyncratic habit of the tree. It will cease to happen when the tree is older. Once established, no maintenance pruning is required.
Special requirements: To train a Davidia, select a single leader and reduce the side shoots, gradually removing them until there is a clear stem of the desired length.

Deutzia

DECIDUOUS SHRUB

General: Deutzias are good summer-flowering shrubs of small to medium size. Pruning follows flowering, when the shoots that have carried flowers are removed almost to their bases. Open up the centre of the bush and cut out shoots that are crowded.
Special requirements: *Deutzia scabra* is a strong upright grower and has the added attraction of an interesting bark. Leave unpruned, carrying out judicious thinning only.

Deutzia 'Montrose'

Elaeagnus
Oleaster

DECIDUOUS/EVERGREEN SHRUB/TREE

General: Fast, strong growing shrubs, a few of them can make small trees. The strongest growers, including the true oleaster (*Elaeagnus angustifolia*) can be trained as small trees by selecting a single leader and well-spaced laterals. Later pruning is to thin and trim. The less vigorous growers are allowed several leaders and trained as shrubs. All Elaeagnus respond well to hard pruning by shooting vigorously from old wood. Deciduous kinds should have their side shoots cut back hard in early spring, and the centres of the bush kept open. Evergreens should be pruned in mid-spring when they may be thinned and trimmed to shape.
Special requirements: As some of the variegated forms have a tendency to revert, any plain green shoots should be removed at their point of origin.

Embothrium
Chilean firebush

EVERGREEN SHRUB/TREE

General: Tender shrubs and trees are noted for their brilliant red flowers in late spring or early summer. Pruning is undesirable and should be confined to correcting misshapen branches after flowering. *Embothrium coccineum* Lanceolatum Group is marginally hardier.
Special requirements: Cut out dead or winter-damaged shoots in early spring.

Enkianthus
Pagoda bush

DECIDUOUS SHRUB

General: This is a choice shrub, noted for its brilliant autumn leaf colour and unusual drooping bell-shaped flowers in spring. *Enkianthus campanulatus* reaches 3m (10ft) high in maturity, and produces reddish twigs when young. Carry out deadheading in late spring, and thin out crowded branches at the same time.
Special requirements: Leggy, overgrown specimens will regenerate if heavily cut back in late winter.

Erica
Heath

EVERGREEN SHRUB

General: Large genus of evergreen shrubs, and similar in many ways to Calluna. Annual pruning is necessary to keep the clumps tidy, compact and floriferous. Using shears, remove old flowers and most of the previous year's growth; the winter and spring flowerers should be clipped after flowering and the summer and autumn flowerers in mid-winter.
Special requirements: Cultivars and species with coloured foliage can, if preferred, be trimmed again just as the flowers form, for it is often the case that the flower and foliage colours will clash. Overgrown tree heaths (*Erica arborea* and *E. terminalis*) should be hard pruned in mid-spring.

Erica x darleyensis 'Kramer's Rote'

Escallonia

EVERGREEN SHRUB

General: Pretty, small, tubular flowers in pink, red or white are carried on shoots from early to late summer, depending on the species. Flowering is on current season's growth and once established, prune hard to within two or three buds of the framework in mid-spring.

Special requirements: In cold districts, and for the definitely tender species such as *Escallonia rubra* var. *macrantha*, wall cultivation is necessary: train a well-spaced fan of branches, and cut back all laterals hard annually in late spring.

Escallonia rubra var. macrantha

Eucalyptus   Gums

EVERGREEN TREE

General: A mass of shoots will be produced on a Eucalyptus sapling, but eventually one shoot will develop more strongly to become a leader whilst the remaining side shoots will die away. Later, branches are shed to leave a clean stem. Eucalyptus has two stages of growth, juvenile and adult; the shape and colour of leaves at each stage may be quite different. Foliage is much in demand by floral arrangers, the juvenile foliage usually being the most popular. Foliage can be cut at any time of year, but excessive cutting should be avoided during the winter. When adult shoots are cut the new ones arising will be juvenile and a tree can be kept in this state indefinitely by regular hard pruning in mid-spring.

Special requirements: *Eucalyptus gunnii* can be coppiced successfully in the smaller garden: cut it down to near ground level in early to mid-spring annually from the second year onwards. This will give it a much more manageable 'bush' shape. Further tipping of vigorous upright shoots may be necessary in mid-summer.

Eucalyptus gunnii

Eucryphia

EVERGREEN SHRUB/TREE

General: This genus comprises trees and shrubs grown for their showy white flowers in late summer. Eucryphias do not take kindly to pruning or training, so you should leave them alone as far as possible.

Special requirements: If, during the spring months, you notice any foliage that has been scorched over winter, you should remove it, along with any stray shoots or branches that mar the plant's symmetry.

Euonymus   Spindle tree

EVERGREEN/DECIDUOUS SHRUB/TREE

General: *Euonymus europaeus* and *E. alatus* are excellent small deciduous trees; they are often primarily grown for their autumn colour and these can be pruned more severely to encourage strong young growth. This is carried out in early spring. Keep the plants to a single leader, the side branches being shortened and gradually removed. The shrubby evergreen kinds, which are grown principally for their glossy and usually variegated foliage, are allowed several leaders. Little pruning is necessary with these, except to thin, trim and keep the centres of the bush open.

Special requirements: The best-known evergreen form is *Euonymus japonicus*, of which there are many variegated forms, some of them very prone to reversion. Trim plant to shape and cut out reverted stems in mid-spring. This species is also prone to attacks by mildew, which can become so bad that normal spraying gives little control. If this happens, severe pruning will remove the unsightly foliage and the new growth will more than likely stay clean.

Euphorbia   Spurge

EVERGREEN SUB-SHRUB

General: Whilst most of this genus is herbaceous, one or two species are woody, and the most noted of these is *Euphorbia characias* subsp. *wulfenii*. After flowering, cut out at ground level all shoots which have flowered and all weak stems. When growth is not strong carry out deadheading and cut out completely some of the oldest stems.

Special requirements: If growing in an exposed position it is best not to carry out drastic pruning in one operation, as this may result in over-thinning and therefore wind damage on the remaining stems. Most Euphorbia species have a milky sap that can irritate sensitive skins.

Euphorbia amygdaloides

Fagus sylvatica 'Purple Fountain'

Fagus
DECIDUOUS TREE   Beech

General: The common beech (*Fagus sylvatica*) is famous as a stately tree in public parks and large gardens. A mature specimen can reach 30m (100ft) or more. Yet young plants may also be trained to grow as a hedge. If growing as a tree, select a central leader and train well-placed branches. Note that Fagus are often slow-growing in the years following planting, but when once established there is plenty of vigour. Trim trees to shape or to size, and trim hedges, in mid-summer.

Special requirements: Weeping varieties are grafted and a leader should be trained up a stake until there is sufficient length of trunk.

x Fatshedera
EVERGREEN SHRUB   Fat-headed lizzie

General: *Fatshedera lizei* is often sold as an indoor plant, but will soon outgrow its container and space. It has a sprawling habit and may be planted outdoors to train up a wall that gets little or no direct sunlight; it can also be used as ground cover. Pruning is rarely necessary, except to remove any dead growth, usually in early spring.

Special requirements: If any all-green leaves appear on variegated forms, remove individually when seen.

Fatsia japonica

Fatsia
EVERGREEN SHRUB   False castor oil plant

General: A handsome, tropical-looking plant with leaves that are glossy, leathery and hand-like with up to nine lobes. Remove dead leaves in spring, or whenever else they are seen, and cut out any bare, gaunt stems at ground level.

Special requirements: Remove any all-green leaves on the variegated form, individually, when seen.

Forsythia
DECIDUOUS SHRUB   Golden bells

General: All pruning should be carried out immediately the golden flowers have faded in late winter or early spring. After planting, reduce the shoots by half or even more; the following winter cut them back to where they begin to curve over. Once a rigid framework has been formed shoots can be allowed to develop freely; subsequent pruning is to remove some or all of the shoots that have flowered. Hard pruning encourages growth at the expense of flowers; so annual pruning should be no more than the removal of crowded shoots from the centre of the bush and a proportion of the oldest wood. When pruning an old or an extra large shrub, spread the operation over three years and begin by removing the oldest wood.

Special requirements: *Forsythia suspensa* is often grown against a wall where its long, pendulous shoots are displayed to best advantage. A well-spaced fan-shaped framework should be trained and tied, and from this will develop the long weeping stems. These should be cut hard back to the framework once the blooms have finished.

Forsythia 'Beatrix Farrand'

Fraxinus
DECIDUOUS TREE   Ash

General: The common ash (*Fraxinus excelsior*) will grow to many tens of metres in height. The Manna ash (*F. ornus*) is noted for its cream flowers in late spring. With both of these, train to a single leader, with well-spaced laterals. Train in a new leader if the original is lost, remembering that because of opposite buds, two will develop where there was one.

Special requirements: Weeping forms, such as *Fraxinus excelsior* 'Pendula', must have the leader tied to a stake; a clear 3.6m (12ft) stem should be produced before a framework is allowed to develop.

Fuchsia 'Dark Eyes'

Fuchsia magellanica

Fuchsia

DECIDUOUS SHRUB

General: In cooler, temperate climates fuchsias are usually grown in pots or containers as greenhouse or conservatory plants, or as temporary outdoor plants for the summer months. A few of the hardier species are able to withstand winters outdoors, but a particularly cold winter can kill off the aboveground growths. Fortunately the bushes usually break away freely from ground level.

Tender fuchsias

To create a fuchsia bush from scratch, the original rooted cutting should be stopped when there are three pairs of leaves. This can result in as many as nine side shoots. Each of the side shoots is then stopped at two pairs of leaves, and this leads to a further four or six side shoots. If you require a really big specimen plant, then a further stopping can be made, again at two pairs of leaves. For this, however, you will need a long growing season, therefore an early start should be made.

Tender fuchsias may also be trained as standards. These can have various lengths of stem but, for most purposes, the stem of a full standard

Fuchsia 'Marinka'

is 80–100cm (30–40in) in height. Other popular shapes include pyramid, fan and espalier.

Hardy fuchsias

Outdoor fuchsias have mostly single flowers of purple and red, but over the years hybridists have introduced shades of white, pink and violet. Some of the hardiest outdoor fuchsias, and also the best, include: 'Alice Hoffman' (pink and white); 'Corallina' (scarlet and purple); 'Lady Thumb'

Fuchsia 'Snowcap'

Fuchsia 'Harry Grey'

(carmine and white); 'Mme Cornelissen' (white and carmine); *Fuchsia magellanica* 'Versicolor' (red and violet, with grey-green leaves tinted pink when young and variegated cream-white); 'Mrs Popple' (scarlet and violet); 'Riccartonii' (red and purple); and 'Tom Thumb' (purple and carmine).

Fuchsia 'Swingtime'

Hardy fuchsias should have previous year's growth cut back to ground level if dead, or back to a good pair of new buds low down on the stem in early spring. Hardy fuchsias can also be grown as low, informal hedges. These should be clipped to shape in spring.

Fuchsia colours

Fuchsia flowers consist of an outer round or tubular calyx with four parts, and a corolla of four inner petals, usually in a different colour. In the descriptions given, the calyx colours are given first.

Garrya
Tassel bush

EVERGREEN SHRUB

General: *Garrya elliptica* is a vigorous evergreen shrub noted for its leathery leaves and conspicuous catkins in late winter and spring. Male and female flowers are produced on different plants and it is the male kind with the long catkins that is most often seen. The female form will produce strings of purple-brown berries in late summer. After training in a well-spaced framework, maintenance pruning consists of thinning and trimming to shape in mid-spring.

Special requirements: Do not prune the female forms if you desire to retain the berries.

Genista
Broom

LEAFLESS SHRUB

Genista lydia

General: Genistas are distinguishable from Cytisus species only by botanists. Consequently they should be grown, and pruned, in exactly the same way. Prune after flowering, cutting back to where new shoots are breaking. Avoid cutting into old wood. At the same time cut out crowded shoots and open up the centre of the bush.

Special requirements: *Genista lydia* can be encouraged to flower more profusely by cutting the flowered shoots back to new stems. The Mount Etna broom (*G. aetnensis*) can be cut back several times each year while young, to make it bushier. Spanish gorse (*G. hispanica*) should be sheared lightly after flowering to tidy it up.

Ginkgo
Maidenhair tree

DECIDUOUS CONIFEROUS TREE

General: This ranks, by appearance alone, as one of the most unlikely looking conifers. Its leaves are broad (fan-shaped), and deciduous. *Ginkgo biloba* is a very tough tree, and is pollution-tolerant. Train to a single leader and well-spaced laterals, taking out strong branches that may develop low down on the tree.

Special requirements: Common to many true conifers there is a tendency for rival leaders to develop when young, and so the strongest only should be selected and trained.

Ginkgo biloba

Gleditsia
Honey locust

DECIDUOUS TREE

General: *Gleditsia triacanthos* is a graceful tree grown for its leaves, which appear late in the spring and which turn golden yellow in autumn. The branches can be brittle, and may break in strong winds. Pruning is not necessary, other than to remove dead wood in the spring. Carry out any other pruning in late summer, as bleeding can occur at other times.

Gleditsia triacanthos

Special requirements: Watch out for the clusters of stout spines growing on the trunk and main branches of this tree.

Griselinia
Broadwood

EVERGREEN SHRUB

General: *Griselinia littoralis* is known for its tolerance of salt air, so is a good choice for coastal gardens. An excellent formal hedging plant, its lime green leaves always seem to look fresh. Trim to shape in mid-spring.

Special requirements: Although Griselinia can be sheared, it is better to use secateurs to remove individual stems, otherwise the foliage is severed and can look unsightly.

Griselinia littoralis

Hamamelis
Witch hazel

DECIDUOUS SHRUB

General: Exquisite, sweetly scented, frost-resistant, long-lasting flowers are produced at the coldest time of year, and there is usually appealing autumn leaf colour. Pruning is generally unnecessary. Most kinds offered for sale are grafted, so watch for suckers; as these closely resemble the desired plant it is best to remove all shoots coming from below ground level.

Special requirements: *Hamamelis japonica* 'Arborea' will make a small tree if it is trained to a single leader.

Hebe

EVERGREEN SHRUB

General: Hebes that flower early in the growing year are pruned after flowering, when all shoots that have carried flowers are cut out. This is also a good time for trimming them to shape and size. Autumn-flowerers are pruned in mid- to late spring; shorten

Hebe 'Margret'

Hibiscus 'Woodbridge'

a few of the longest shoots and thin as necessary. The hardy kinds need little attention except a trimming to shape in mid-spring.

Special requirements: Sometimes hebes will die back for no accountable reason, first one shoot, then another. Little can be done to halt this decline; you can cut out the dying stems, but this often results in an unshapely eyesore. At this stage you should replace with a young plant.

Hedera   Ivy
EVERGREEN CLIMBER

General: Ivy can be invasive and if left unattended can dislodge slates, gutters and down pipes. Controversy rages as to whether it is harmful to a tree when growing up it. As long as the tree is in good health, no damage is done. Likewise, if the brickwork of the wall is sound, and the pipes and guttering also, there should be no damage. Having said this, it is advisable to cut stems from windows, doors, pipes, gutters and the roof.

Ivy has two stages of growth: the juvenile, with angular leaves and climbing roots, and the later stage when side branches without roots are produced, leaves become rounder and flowering takes place. It can be slow to start climbing up a wall. Train a well-balanced framework, and where tying in is possible (such as on a trellis) try to clothe the area with leaves and stems, especially at the base. If branches grow outwards from the structure up which the plant is climbing, cut them back close to it. Each year cut out some of the oldest wood; this will help to ensure that the ivy does not become so heavy that it falls away from the wall.

Special requirements: It is only on young shoots that roots develop which adhere to the wall and if these die or are wrenched away, there is no hold.

Hibiscus   Tree hollyhock
DECIDUOUS SHRUB

General: This is mainly a tropical genus; only one species, *Hibiscus syriacus*, is commonly seen in gardens in temperate countries. The funnel-shaped flowers are carried on current season's growth. Once a framework has been trained, all young shoots should be cut back to within a few buds of it around mid-spring.

Special requirements: Coral spot fungus can be troublesome, especially if the shrub is weak.

Hippophaë   Sea buckthorn
DECIDUOUS SHRUB/TREE

General: As its common name suggests, a good plant for coastal gardens. Its dense, spiny growth also makes it fine for hedging. To obtain the bright orange berries plants should be set out in groups, with one male to several females. Little pruning is required except to trim and thin during the dormant season. Hedges may be trimmed to shape and size in summer.

Special requirements: Though most often grown as shrubs, they make small trees if trained to a single leader with the lower side shoots reduced.

Hydrangea
EVERGREEN/DECIDUOUS SHRUB/CLIMBER

General: Hydrangeas often take a year or two to settle down before they start to flower regularly in summer and autumn. One facet of the hydrangea, common through the genus, is that it will grow freely from the base, allowing you to prune out old and worn branches, even from the species and cultivars that are not normally pruned.

Hydrangea macrophylla

Bush forms
Hydrangea macrophylla is the common hydrangea, its cultivars often referred to as Hortensia (mop-head) or Lacecap hydrangeas. They flower on one-year-old wood, and pruning consists of removing all or part of the shoot that has flowered, and cutting out any weak shoots.

Climbing forms
These attach themselves to their support by means of roots, and as with ivy there are two stages – juvenile growth, with climbing roots, that clings tight to its support. In the adult stage, branches develop which have no roots and these carry flowers. Cut these flowering shoots hard back in mid-spring.

Tree-like forms
H. paniculata is tree-like with a semi-arching habit, growing to at least 3.5m (12ft). It flowers in summer on current season's growth, which is cut hard back to two buds of the framework during early spring.

Special requirements: Young growths of all hydrangeas can be caught by late spring frosts, and any damaged growths should be pruned back.

Hypericum — St John's wort
DECIDUOUS SHRUB

General: All garden hypericums are characterised by their saucer-shaped yellow flowers with central clusters of prominent stamens. A few species are tender. Blooms are carried on current season's growth, therefore to get the best flowers on compact plants it is best in mid-spring to cut all shoots back to within 5–8cm (2–3in) of the ground. Thinning and tipping the younger growth can be carried out to create larger plants.
Special requirements: *Hypericum* x *inodorum* 'Elstead' is susceptible to damage by rust fungus; infected shoots should be cut out and burned.

Ilex — Holly
EVERGREEN/DECIDUOUS SHRUB/TREE

General: Hollies are often slow to establish but, having done so, grow away strongly. The strong growers, which are to become trees, should have a single leader selected but all side shoots retained until they die naturally. Pruning consists of trimming to shape in mid-spring. Straggly or overgrown shrubs may be cut back hard in mid- or late spring. Hedges should be trimmed back in mid-summer.
Special requirements: Neglected hollies or those disfigured by the leaf miner insect pest can be cut back in mid-spring or in mid-summer.

Ilex aquifolium 'Golden Queen'

Juglans — Walnut

see page 123

Juniperus — Juniper
EVERGREEN CONIFER

General: The forms making trees should be trained to a central leader, with all side shoots retained. The bushes can have several leaders. Dwarf and prostrate junipers are not pruned.
Special requirements: It is important to allow the bushy junipers sufficient space and light for healthy growth, otherwise the build-up of dead material among the branch systems makes them unsightly. In mid-spring the centres should be cleared of the clutter of shoots, both dead and alive.

Juniperus scopulorum 'Skyrocket'

Kalmia latifolia 'Pink Charm'

Kalmia — Calico bush
EVERGREEN SHRUB

General: *Kalmia latifolia* is plant that loves acid soil. Less commonly seen is *K. angustifolia* f. *rubra*, known as the sheep laurel. Slow growing, they both produce flowers in late spring and early summer. Very little pruning is required, except for deadheading.
Special requirements: When bushes become straggly, over-large or there is too much old wood, hard pruning can be carried out during mid-spring. Reducing the size of large specimens should be carried out over a 3–5 year period.

Kerria — Jew's mallow
DECIDUOUS SHRUB

General: *Kerria japonica* makes an attractive, early flowering bush, with bright green stems. Blooms are carried on the previous year's growth. Cut out old

Laburnum
Golden chain or Golden rain

DECIDUOUS TREE

General: Laburnums are most commonly grown as standards, for which they are well suited. Strong vertical shoots tend to appear from low down on the tree and these should be removed as they appear. Laburnum responds well to spur pruning so that trees can be restricted in size by cutting back side shoots to two or three buds in the winter. Laburnum is well suited to pleaching: several famous large gardens boast ancient 'laburnum arches' – tunnels which for a couple of weeks every year in late spring come alive with golden flowers.

Special requirements: Laburnums seed heavily and the immature seedpods should be removed, especially as the seed is poisonous.

canes at ground level as flowers fade.

Special requirements: Kerria has a suckering habit, forming large clumps, which may need to be restricted.

Kolkwitzia
Beauty bush

DECIDUOUS SHRUB

General: *Kolkwitzia amabilis* is grown for its pink and yellow foxglove-shaped flowers and peeling bark, attractive in winter. Leave to develop naturally, except for the thinning of shoots where crowded. If, however, space is limited, annual pruning can be carried out in early summer when shoots that have flowered may be removed.

Special requirements: Old, overgrown bushes may be renovated: leave five to seven strong, young, healthy stems, but remove all other growth.

Larix
Larch

DECIDUOUS CONIFER

General: Larix is the largest genus of deciduous conifers, but because the 'foliage' comprises very thin needles, the trees cast only a light shade. Select a single leader, replacing it if damaged by bad weather or insect or mammal pests. Retain all side branches as long as possible. Prune when fully dormant.

Special requirements: Late pruning results in excessive gumming.

Laurus
Bay

EVERGREEN SHRUB/TREE

General: *Laurus nobilis* is an aromatic plant from the Mediterranean region. Laurus can be trimmed to form a pyramidal or rounded dense shrub, or a central leader can be retained to turn it into a single-stemmed tree. Clip formal specimens to shape and trim hedge in mid-spring and again if required in late summer.

Special requirements: Frost-damaged shoots should be removed in spring, cutting back to sound wood.

Lavandula — Lavender
EVERGREEN SHRUB

General: Common lavender is frequently seen in gardens as an untidy, sprawling bush, and this is due entirely to lack of pruning. During mid-spring, just prior to growth commencing, bushes should be clipped hard, in the course of which old flower spikes are removed and most of the previous year's growth, and any winter damage. Neglected bushes can be hard-pruned to renovate them, but it is better done in two or three stages rather than all at once.
Special requirements: A few species, including the popular French lavender (*Lavandula stoechas*), are tender and need the protection of a warm south wall.

Lavatera — Tree mallow
DECIDUOUS SHRUB

General: The shrubby *Lavatera olbia* is a bushy, upright plant with rich green stems and wide purplish pink flowers from mid-summer to late autumn. Cut back all stems to within 30cm (12in) of the ground when shoots are bursting into growth in mid-spring.
Special requirements: It is slightly tender plant, needing full sun and a rather poor, well-drained soil.

Leycesteria — Himalayan honeysuckle or Pheasant berry
DECIDUOUS SHRUB

General: The most common species, *Leycesteria formosa*, is semi-tender and only suited to a warm, sunny wall; but if cold weather cuts back growth new shoots grow readily from the base. It is grown for its maroon and white flowers and red-purple berries. The old stems should be cut out in mid-spring. If growth is strong, the entire clump can be cut down to ground level each year.
Special requirements: In an exposed, windy garden the stems, being hollow, can be broken by strong winds; these should be cut out immediately.

Ligustrum — Privet
EVERGREEN/DECIDUOUS SHRUB

General: Privets are best known as hedging plants though specimens are sometimes used in topiary; the best for this purpose is *Ligustrum ovalifolium*. Privet can also make handsome freestanding shrubs or even, with some stretch of the imagination, small trees. Shrubs are left to develop several leaders and established pruning consists of trimming to shape and thinning in early spring. Hedges need clipping two or three times in the growing season.
Special requirements: Strong-growing ligustrums, such as *L. lucidum* and its forms, can be trained to a single leader with all its side shoots retained but shortened.

Liquidambar — Sweet gum
DECIDUOUS TREE

General: *Liquidambar styraciflua* is one of the best trees for autumn leaf colouring. Select a strong central leader and well-spaced laterals. Strong

Liquidambar styraciflua 'Lane Roberts'

branches can occur low down on the tree and these should be removed.
Special requirements: *L. formosana* and its various forms are liable to be injured by late spring frosts; cut away any damaged growth when seen.

Liriodendron   Tulip tree

DECIDUOUS TREE

General: *Liriodendron tulipifera* is a tall, stately tree with both tulip-shaped leaves and blooms. To train a young tree select a central leader and well-spaced side branches. Training and subsequent pruning is best carried out during mid- to late summer.
Special requirements: Note that the bark is easily damaged if blunt tools are used and such wood tends to die back.

Liriodendron tulipefera

Lonicera   Honeysuckle or Woodbine

DECIDUOUS/EVERGREEN SHRUB/CLIMBER

General: Best known as highly fragrant-flowered climbing plants, there are also shrubby forms and an evergreen species used for formal hedges. It is not necessary to prune the climbing forms every year, unless space is restricted in the garden. The climbers can be separated into two groups: those flowering on one-year-old wood (such as the common *Lonicera periclymenum*) are pruned after flowering when those shoots which have flowered are removed, together with crowded growth; and those flowering on current season's wood (such as *L. japonica*) are pruned in the winter, when necessary, cutting back hard to a framework. Shrubby honeysuckles (including the winter-flowering *L. fragrantissima*, and *L. nitida*, good for hedging) should be trimmed to shape after flowering, and branches that have carried the blooms should be cut back or removed completely.
Special requirements: If you want to let the plant produce their berries, pruning should be delayed until the winter, or mid-spring for evergreens.

Lupinus   Lupin

EVERGREEN SHRUB

General: The best known shrubby lupin is *Lupinus arboreus*. In spring shorten some of the youngest wood, and cut out completely some of the oldest and weakest wood. Deadhead in late summer.
Special requirements: When deadheading, leave sufficient heads for seed production if you fancy trying your hand at propagation, particularly as this lupin is short-lived, lasting only a few years.

Magnolia

DECIDUOUS/EVERGREEN SHRUB/TREE

General: The wood of magnolias tends to be pithy and bark is easily damaged if blunt or badly set tools are used. Pruning is best carried out in mid-summer when new growth is complete: dormant wood is slow to heal and dieback following winter pruning is common. Tree magnolias should be kept to a single leader. Young growth is frequently damaged by late frosts and if the leader is destroyed a new one will have to be trained in. In general, overgrown or wind-damaged magnolias regenerate well if cut back in mid-summer.
Special requirements: *Magnolia grandiflora* is considered by many to be a wall shrub, but it is really unsuitable in such a position for its large leaves cause undue shading, and old stems are difficult to tie back. It may produce more flowers in such a position, however. Wall training can be in a fan, or in tiers, ensuring that the base of the wall is kept clothed. Thin and cut back shoots coming from the wall in mid-summer. The most popular of the smaller magnolias is *M. stellata*. Allow it to grow naturally – as a specimen shrub in a lawn, perhaps – but as it ages it may spread beyond its allocated space. If this happens, cut back some of the oldest branches to their base, in mid-summer.

Lupinus arboreus

Mahonia japonica 'Bealei'

Mahonia — Oregon grape

EVERGREEN SHRUB

General: *Mahonia aquifolium* is the true Oregon grape but *M. japonica* is the most commonly grown form; both are winter flowering with prickly leaves. Mahonias need only occasional pruning when the oldest stems can be cut out at ground level in mid-spring.

Special requirements: If a plant is weak, remove some of the oldest stems and trim back the remaining growth. Then feed with a good balanced shrub fertilizer.

Malus — Crab apple

DECIDUOUS TREE

General: These trees are grown for their ornamental miniature apples and showy spring flowers. Some forms are raised from seed and therefore on their own roots, but many are grafted on to one of the

Malus 'Evereste'

fruit rootstocks which controls the ultimate size of the tree (see page 95). Crab apples are generally grown as standards. Once the framework has formed, there is little pruning required beyond the removal of suckers and any crossing branches (see pages 102–3).

Special requirements: Unlike fruiting apples which are spur pruned, the ornamental Malus do not respond well to hard pruning.

Olearia — Daisy bush

EVERGREEN SHRUB/TREE

General: Olearia bear clusters of white, daisy-like flowers in summer. Most species are tender and often planted as freestanding shrubs at the foot of a wall. Forms that bloom early in the year are pruned after the flowers have faded, when old flowered shoots are removed and the plant is trimmed to shape. Those flowering late are pruned in late spring, again removing old flower stalks and trimming to shape.

Special requirements: *Olearia nummulariifolia* sometimes has a tendency to spread outwards, encroaching on neighbouring plants; pruning in mid-spring can rectify this.

Olearia macrodonta

Osmanthus

EVERGREEN SHRUB/TREE

General: Most species are slow-growing, and produce strongly fragrant white flowers. They can be damaged in cold winters, or if grown in exposed positions. *Osmanthus delavayi* and *O. heterophyllus* are the hardiest, the former flowering in spring, the latter in late autumn. The early flowerers are trimmed after flowering, the late flowerers in late

spring just before growth begins.
Special requirements: *Osmanthus* x *burkwoodii*, which can also be grown as a formal hedge, should be trimmed to shape in late spring, after flowering.

Pachysandra
Japanese spurge

EVERGREEN SHRUB

General: These spreading sub-shrubs form prostrate carpets, and produce inconspicuous spikes of white or pinkish flowers in early spring. Pruning is only required if the foliage becomes thin or the stems become bare and woody. In mid-spring, after the flowers have finished, shear the stems off 5–8cm (2–3in) above ground level.
Special requirements: The variegated form, *Pachysandra terminalis* 'Variegata', may produce the occasional all-green leaf. Remove these when seen.

Paeonia
Tree peony

DECIDUOUS SHRUB

General: *Paeonia delavayi*, *P. lutea* and *P. suffruticosa* are all woody species. Take out some of the old stems at ground level if they become lanky with sparse foliage. If the summer has been wet, it is advantageous to thin out some of the lush new growth; this allows autumn sunshine to ripen the wood and encourage better flowering the next year.
Special requirements: Deadheading should be practised, but if seeds are wanted, delay the task until they have been shed.

Parrotia
Persian ironwood

DECIDUOUS SHRUB

General: Grown mainly for its dramatic autumn leaf tints, *Parrotia persica* also boasts early flowers and colourful bark. A central leader may be trained with all side shoots retained, or it can be allowed to develop naturally.

Special requirements: Parrotia produces masses of branches, which may be thinned following flowering, cutting back to their points of origin, but most experts recommend leaving the tree to its own devices.

Paulownia tomentosa (coppiced)

Parrotia persica

Parthenocissus
Virginia creeper

DECIDUOUS CLIMBER

General: *Parthenocissus quinquefolia* and its close relations are vigorous climbers which attach themselves to supports by means of tendrils on which there are suckers. Unless given plenty of space, they can be invasive. Where possible, an annual reduction of growth is desirable, at least so as to avoid the dislodging of roof tiles or blocking windows. Cut out old wood, remembering that it is only young shoots which are able to attach themselves to supports. *See also Ampelopsis, page 60.*

Special requirements: All pruning should be carried out in mid-winter, when there is no danger of the plant bleeding.

Paulownia

DECIDUOUS TREE

General: A well-grown *Paulownia tomentosa* in full flower is simply spectacular. It is fast growing when young, producing shoots that are easily damaged by cold. Flower buds are formed in the autumn but many will drop off over winter; in late spring the survivors open spikes of mauve, foxglove-like blooms. It is only in the mildest parts that regular flowering can be expected, so the tree is often grown for its foliage. Train to a central leader and well-spaced laterals. Little maintenance pruning is needed: after flowering, remove any winter damage and dead wood, and thin out if required.

Special requirements: Sometimes, particularly during wet years, rival leaders are created; remove these when seen.

Perovskia
Russian sage

DECIDUOUS SHRUB

General: Blue flowers are carried on long stems in late summer, giving these shrubs a look almost like straggly lavenders from a distance. Shoots often die back in the winter, which does not matter as flowers are produced on current season's growth. Therefore all shoots should be cut back to ground level in early spring.

Special requirements: Old or neglected plants respond well to this hard pruning.

Perovskia atriplicifolia 'Blue Spire'

Philadelphus

Mock orange

DECIDOUS SHRUB

General: Showy, freely produced white flowers adorn the branches in summer, and most of them give off a powerful scent of orange blossom. Philadelphus can be grown with the minimum of pruning, limited perhaps to the removal of surplus shoots and any non-flowering shoots from the centre of the shrub. Where space is limited, after the flowers have faded, remove branches that have carried blooms and thin out surplus shoots. All pruning should be carried out in mid-summer.
Special requirements: *Philadelphus coronarius* 'Aureus' and 'Variegatus' are grown mainly for their golden or variegated leaves. The best colouring is found on the younger wood, so it is important to maintain a good proportion of this each year.

Philadelphus coronarius 'Aureus'

Phlomis

Jerusalem sage

EVERGREEN SHRUB

General: There are several herbaceous and shrubby forms of Phlomis available but only one, *Phlomis fruticosa*, is grown widely. Remove or cut back old flowering stems, and thin overcrowded wood, in spring.
Special requirements: The leafy shoot tips are soft and liable to damage by severe winter weather; prune out any damaged growths when seen.

Phlomis fruticosa

Photinia 'Red Robin'

Photinia

EVERGREEN SHRUB

General: Small white flowers appear in spring, followed by small red fruits, but the main attraction is the red colouring of the new leaves each spring. In mid-spring all growth should be trimmed back to about half of that produced in the previous year.
Special requirements: Some photinias, including *Photinia davidiana*, can be tender and are best grown against a sunny wall.

Picea

Spruce

EVERGREEN CONIFER

General: The spruces are 'monopodal'; that is, they should have a single stem and only light side branching. They require no regular pruning regime, other than, when young, to select and retain a central leader. If you have to, just lightly trim the tips of the branches, cutting only in to areas of existing green foliage.
Special requirements: Sunlight should be able to reach the centre of the plant, so keep the immediate surround clear of shrub growth

Pieris

Lily-of-the-Valley bush

EVERGREEN SHRUB

General: The waxy, white flowers appear in spring, along with brilliant pink and red emerging leaves. Little pruning is needed, except to deadhead, thin and trim the shrub. It is important to remove shoot tips that have been damaged by winter frosts. If left, these could lead to die-back.
Special requirements: A second flush of coloured foliage can be achieved by trimming back the first flush shoots when the leaves have turned green.

Pieris 'Flaming Silver'

Pinus

Pino

EVERGREEN CONIFER

General: Pine trees are thought by some to be the largest group of tree on the planet. Each cluster of pine needles represents a short shoot and has a small, dormant bud in the centre: this only grows if the shoot tip is damaged. Pruning, which should simply be a matter of removing damaged branches, should be done when fully dormant to avoid excessive gumming.

Special requirements: Some of the naturally dwarf pines, such as *Pinus pumila*, produce several leaders, but in general all species should be kept to a single leader.

Platanus hispanica

Pinus sylvestris 'Fastigiata'

leader and well-spaced laterals, aiming to produce a clear trunk of 4.5m (15ft), with a well-balanced and spaced framework.

Special requirements: *Platanus orientalis* is a strong grower, but old wood on specimens beyond their prime is prone to developing cavities. This means that, to avoid the loss of large branches, old trees should be braced as a precaution.

Pittosporum

EVERGREEN SHRUB

General: Originating from the warmest parts of New Zealand, most species of Pittosporum are tender, *Pittosporum tenuifolium* being the hardiest. Plant it in a protected place out of cold winds. Trim to shape in mid-spring, cutting out winter damage; thin at the same time. Although they do not need hard pruning generally, pittosporums do regenerate freely from old wood.

Special requirements: *P. ralphii* makes a spreading bush, and may be pruned in spring to encourage a more compact habit.

Pittosporum 'Silver Queen'

Platanus

Plane

DECIDUOUS TREE

General: The planes are fast-growing trees, commonly used in street planting. Given plenty of space and time, they become graceful trees with branches sweeping to the ground. Select a central

Populus

Poplar

DECIDUOUS TREE

General: Tall, stately poplars are traditionally used as windbreaks in parks and open spaces, but there are many smaller forms for garden use as well. Most species are strong growers, especially when young. To train, select a central leader and well-spaced laterals. Take care not to damage roots otherwise suckering occurs. No regular pruning regime is required. If pruning is considered necessary, though, carry it out in the dormant period otherwise bleeding may result.

Special requirements: As canker disease, causing dieback and gumming, can be troublesome, all pruning cuts should be paired to avoid exposed, torn wood, the presence of which makes it easier for disease to enter.

Potentilla

Cinquefoil

DECIDUOUS SHRUB

General: Perennial potentillas are good plants for rock gardens, whilst the shrubby types are excellent ground coverers; both make fine border plants. *Potentilla fruticosa* is the common shrubby form,

Populus lasiocarpa

Prunus lusitanica

and produces saucer-shaped flowers in summer, in colours ranging from white and yellow through to orange, pink and red. During early spring reduce the previous year's growth by half.

Special requirements: Potentillas are untidy growers that tend to collect dead leaves and accumulate a mass of twigs. To keep the plants healthy, clear out the centres of bushes when you do the main cutting back.

Potentilla 'Primrose Beauty'

Prunus

DECIDUOUS/EVERGREEN SHRUB/TREE

General: This is a large genus with many types of tree and shrub of differing size, shape and habit. Those that make trees are trained to a central leader with well-spaced laterals. Japanese flowering cherries are grafted; if suckering occurs, therefore, remove them before they dominate the tree. Weeping cherries are popular; support the main stem with a stake and ensure that there is sufficient length of trunk to allow the pendant branches to hang gracefully. The evergreen species, most commonly the cherry laurel (*Prunus laurocerasus*) and the Portugal laurel (*P. lusitanica*), can be grown as specimen plants, but they also make good, dense hedges. Retain side shoots, and trim these to shape

in mid-spring. Pruning of most other species is kept to a minimum after building up a framework.

Special requirements: Some kinds, such as *P. serrula*, are grown for their barks. Train a central leader and well-spaced laterals, so as to expose the trunk as clearly as possible.

See also relevant entries in this book on the pruning of plums, damsons and gages (pages 107–8), cherries (pages 109–10), peaches, nectarines and apricots (pages 111–12), and almonds (page 123).

Pyracantha   Firethorn

EVERGREEN SHRUB

General: These evergreen shrubs have spiny branches, bright, small summer flowers, and prolific autumn berries. They make fine shady wall shrubs and hedging plants. During training select several leaders, spacing them well apart. Freestanding pyracanthas should have three or five well spaced leaders. In mid-spring open up the centre of the bush, thin out crowded shoots and trim to shape. The main leaders of wall-trained types should be secured in position, for though they keep close to the wall they tend to fall away with age. During mid-spring, cut back any shoots coming away from the wall, thin out crowded shoots and trim back.

Special requirements: Be careful of the plant's spines when pruning: wear stout gloves, thick clothing and goggles.

Pyracantha 'Teton'

Quercus rubra

Rhododendron 'Pink Pearl'

Rhus typhina

Ribes speciosum

Quercus Oak

DECIDUOUS/EVERGREEN TREE

General: Just a few oaks are suitable for the average garden. Train these to a central leader and well-spaced laterals. Ensure that the main limbs are well spaced and give a good shape to the crown. Some evergreen oaks may suffer damage in cold winters and trimming may be necessary in late spring to remove affected leaves and stems.
Special requirements: The holm oak (*Quercus ilex*) can be clipped to form a striking hedge.

Rhododendron

DECIDUOUS/EVERGREEN SHRUB

General: Azaleas, which form a large part of the Rhododendron genus, are included here. Do not plant rhododendrons too deeply, as this can cause the plant to appear sickly, and parts of it may die. Many forms are grafted, so any suckers arising from the rootstsock should be removed as they appear. Carry out deadheading annually and at the same time trim back any shoots growing out of alignment. If a rhododendron becomes too tall, bare at the base, or its shape falls away, it can usually be cut back hard once flowering is over.
Special requirements: Bud blast can appear as a dark brown colouration of the bud, usually with fungal pustules along the surface. Remove and burn infected buds.

Rhus Sumach

DECIDUOUS SHRUB/TREE

General: The form most often seen in gardens is the stag's horn sumach (*Rhus typhina*), grown mainly for its bright red autumn foliage. Handling some species can cause a skin rash. Keep tree forms to a single leader and well-spaced branches. Shrubs can be left unpruned, thinning out crowded shoots in early spring.
Special requirements: Suckering can become a problem, and a single plant can throw up a sucker quite a distance away from the trunk.

Ribes Flowering currants

DECIDUOUS/EVERGREEN SHRUB

General: The most popular ornamental Ribes is *Ribes sanguineum* which produces pink flowers in mid-spring. Most forms bloom on one-year-old wood, and after flowering the shoots that have carried the flowers are cut back. During the winter, open up the centre of the bush and cut back young growth to within two or three buds of the main stems. Evergreen kinds are little pruned except to thin, if required, in mid-spring.
Special requirements: Ornamental Ribes can be grown as loose, informal hedging. Cut back annually, after flowering, but do so selectively, for shearing is likely to impair flowering the following year.
See also blackcurrants (page 128), red and white currants (page 129) and gooseberries (page 130).

Robinia pseudoacacia 'Frisia'

Robinia — False acacia

DECIDUOUS TREE

General: This tree has a graceful shape, bright yellow-green leaves and pea-like whitish flowers in late spring. It also has thorns and produces suckers freely if the roots are damaged. The wood can be brittle, and it is not unusual for trees to shed large limbs in heavy wind. Train a single leader and well-spaced laterals.

Special requirements: Cut out any vigorous shoots that develop low down on the tree, for these will spoil the ultimate shape.

Rosmarinus — Rosemary

EVERGREEN SHRUB

General: Whilst reasonably hardy, rosemary may suffer in very cold weather. Trim bushes to shape in mid-spring, but wait until after the first flush of the pale blue flowers has finished.

Special requirements: Low growing forms, if in exposed positions, can be severely damaged in even an averagely cold winter.

Rubus — Ornamental brambles

DECIDUOUS/EVERGREEN

General: There are several excellent garden species of Rubus, grown mainly for their flowers, foliage and colourful winter stems. Most have a suckering habit, and others (like blackberries) have canes of only two year's duration. The best known ornamental bramble is *Rubus cockburnianus*, with white winter stems: cut the oldest canes to ground level in early spring, and thin out remaining young growth in established clumps.

Special requirements: Species grown for their flowers or fruit are pruned during the winter. *See also* blackberries, loganberries and hybrids (page 125–6), and raspberries (pages 126–7).

Ruta — Rue

EVERGREEN SHRUB

General: A small genus of slightly tender, short-lived sub-shrubs; common rue (*Ruta graveolens*) is grown for its blue-grey strongly aromatic foliage. Often considered to be an untidy grower, it can endure, and probably deserves, drastic trimming and thinning in late spring.

Special requirements: 'Jackman's Blue' is a compact form of *R. graveolens*, requiring less drastic pruning.

Salix gracilistyla 'Melanostachys'

Salix — Willow

DECIDUOUS SHRUB/TREE

General: Willows vary from large trees to small garden shrubs but all prefer moist soil. Tree forms are trained to a single leader and well-spaced laterals; shrubs can be similarly treated but with all side shoots retained. Multi-stemmed forms (such as forms of *Salix alba* that are grown for their winter stem colour), should be cut to ground level, or to within a few buds of a framework, in early spring Low-growing and prostrate willows are rarely pruned, except to thin and cut out dead wood.

Special requirements: With large, mature trees there is a tendency for branches to snap or fall in high wind, so it is important to avoid creating narrow (weak) crotches, and unnecessarily long limbs.

Salvia — Sage

DECIDUOUS/EVERGREEN SHRUB

General: Common sage (*Salvia officinalis*) is widely grown in the herb garden and used in cooking, though coloured leaf forms may be grown purely for ornamental purposes. There are two groups of common sage: those that flower rarely and others that flower freely. The former should be trimmed to shape in mid-spring, removing any flowering stems. With the latter, during late spring cut out all flowered shoots and trim to shape.

Special requirements: The tender kinds, which include the popular *S. elegans* 'Scarlet Pineapple', should be planted near the base of a sunny wall; any growth that survives the winter should be cut hard back in spring.

Salvia microphylla 'Maraschino'

Sambucus · Elder
DECIDUOUS SHRUB

General: These hardy shrubs are grown for their clusters of flowers, fruits and attractive, finely cut leaves. During winter cut out old wood and any weak shoots, open up the centre and trim back young shoots. Elders with fancy leaves can have two-year stems cut to ground level and one year stems reduced by half. Old, leggy shrubs may be cut back to ground level in winter to induce a more compact shape.

Special requirements: *Sambucus nigra* 'Albovariegata' with mottled leaves may be trained as a small standard, with up to 2m (6ft) of clear stem. Remove any suckers as soon as they are seen.

Sambucus nigra

Santolina · Cotton lavender
EVERGREEN SHRUB

General: *Santolina chamaecyparissus* is a hardy, aromatic shrub grown for its grey-white foliage. *S. pinnata* subsp. *neapolitana* is slightly taller, more open and with larger leaves. If you do not prune these at all, the bushes are short-lived and sprawl untidily. So, after flowering at the end of summer, remove old flower stems and trim back the bushes.

Special requirements: If growing just for foliage, trim in mid-spring and remove most of the previous year's growth; a second trimming is desirable as the flower buds appear in early summer.

Sarcococca · Christmas box or Sweet box
EVERGREEN SHRUB

General: A slow-growing hardy shrub with glossy green leaves and fragrant white flowers from early to late winter. Most commonly grown forms are

Santolina chamaecyparissus

Sarcococca confusa, which reaches to 1.5m (5ft) in 10 years or so, and *S. hookeriana* var. *digyna*, which reaches a little over half this height. Trim the shrubs back if they are becoming invasive; otherwise just cut out old, gaunt stems. *S. hookeriana* will sometimes throw out strong, upright growths, much higher than the rest; cut these back when seen.

Special requirements: If clumps become untidy, shear back to around 30cm (12in) of ground level in mid-spring.

Senecio
EVERGREEN SHRUB

General: Although the genus Brachyglottis is now botanically correct for this shrub, it is still best known under the names *Senecio greyii*, *S. laxifolius* or *S.* 'Sunshine'. Not fully hardy in severe winters, it grows very happily against a sunny wall. In late spring remove any winter damage and thin out crowded shoots. At the same time trim to shape, thin, and remove the old flower stalks.

Special requirements: To keep plants fresh, and to prolong their lives, prune back hard every four years, to perhaps 30–45cm (12–18in) from the ground. Plants will look unhappy for a time but will be better for it once new growth starts again.

Skimmia
EVERGREEN SHRUB

General: Slow-growing, hardy shrubs suited to small gardens. Male and female flowers are carried on separate plants, so both sexes need to be grown in close proximity for autumn berries. If necessary, trim to shape in mid-spring, and occasionally remove some of the oldest wood.

Special requirements: Do not plant Skimmia close to a wall or pathway, as cutting back is difficult to do without spoiling the shape and overall 'surface' of the plant.

Skimmia japonica

Solanum — Chilean potato tree
SEMI-EVERGREEN SHRUB/CLIMBER

General: A woody climbing shrub, *Solanum crispum* is the most commonly seen form, with lilac and yellow flowers from early summer until early autumn. They can be vigorous and need drastic annual pruning in late spring, when the previous year's shoots may be reduced by half. All excess shoots should be removed entirely.

Special requirements: For completely clothing a wall with *S. jasminoides*, use a system of horizontal and vertical wires and tie shoots in regularly.

Sorbus — Mountain ash, Rowan and Whitebeam
DECIDUOUS SHRUB/TREE

General: Mountain ashes and rowans have small opposite leaflets on long leaf stalks, often colouring brilliantly in autumn, with berries in several different shades. Species include *Sorbus aucuparia*, *S. hupehensis* and *S.* 'Joseph Rock'. Whitebeams have much larger, single leaves, often white-felted underneath, and are represented by *S. aria* and *S. thibetica* 'John Mitchell'. Train both types to a single leader with well-spaced laterals. Once a framework has formed, you may occasionally need to cut out a crossing branch.

Special requirements: When trees carry large crops of berries, the sheer weight of fruit can pull branches out of shape; early spring pruning may be necessary to correct this. Most Sorbus are susceptible to fireblight, and diseased branches should be cut out as soon as they are seen.

Spiraea
DECIDUOUS SHRUB

General: Some species, such as *Spiraea japonica* and *S. douglasii* flower on current year's growth and are pruned to within 2–3cm (5–8in) of ground level during late winter. Other species flower on one-year wood, such as *S.* x *vanhouttei* and *S.* 'Arguta'; these are cut back after flowering is finished, to where new growth is emerging. All spireas can be used as decorative informal hedging.

Special requirements: *Spiraea japonica* 'Bullata' is a close, compact grower, and only needs to be sheared over in spring. Do not cut too far into the older wood.

Symphoricarpos — Snowberry
DECIDUOUS SHRUB

General: This shrub comes alive in autumn with masses of pure white berries. All species have a suckering habit which can be invasive in a good soil. During early spring, remove the oldest and weakest shoots, thinning the remainder.

Special requirements: To curb the invasive nature of Symphoricarpos, plant against a hard edge, such as a road, or a concrete-sided trench.

Syringa — Common lilac
DECIDUOUS SHRUB/TREE

General: Little pruning is required, except for the removal of blind shoots from the centre of bushes, and deadheading in late summer. If space is tight you should trim back some of the shoots at the same time. The stronger kinds, such as *Syringa vulgaris* and its many forms, will make small trees if kept to a single leader, and trained; however, this will need regular attention because of the forking habit of lilac.

Special requirements: Most cultivars are grafted on to either a form of wild lilac, or on to privet; suckers from both stocks are likely, and they should be removed when seen.

Tamarix — Tamarisk

DECIDUOUS SHRUB/TREE

General: The feathery foliage of these shrubs looks delicate, yet it is able to withstand heavy wind extremely well, making them ideal for coastal gardens. Some, such as *Tamarix tentandra* and *T. parviflora*, flower on one-year-old wood in late spring, and these should be pruned following flowering, the wood that has flowered being cut out and the resulting growths thinned. Others, like *T. pentandra*, flower in late summer and these are pruned hard in early spring; some thinning of growths at the same time may be desirable.

Special requirements: The strongest kinds can be trained into small trees by selecting a central leader and reducing side shoots.

Taxus — Yew

EVERGREEN CONIFER

General: Trees are trained to a central leader with all side branches retained. Bush forms can be similarly trained, but the leading shoot should be stopped at the desired height, and here also several leaders can be allowed to grow. Some trimming to shape in mid-spring of these kinds may be necessary, when the centre of the bush should be cleared of dead foliage and sticks. Often several leaders are allowed but with age these tend to fall apart and some unobtrusive tying together of main stems in necessary to retain shape.

Special requirements: Irish yew (*Taxus baccata* 'Fastigiata') can be trained to a central leader, but the resulting tree may be too slender and require staking.

Thuja — Arbor-vitae

EVERGREEN CONIFER

General: This is a genus of hardy, slow-growing conifers that make fine specimen trees, according to size, for large or small gardens. Little pruning is needed, other than to select and retain a single leader; retain all side branches. Small-growing and dwarf forms are left unpruned.

Special requirements: Some trimming to shape may be necessary in mid-spring.

Tilia — Lime or Linden

DECIDUOUS TREE

General: Tilias are vigorous trees needing plenty of space. Select a single leader and well-spaced laterals, training a well-spaced and balanced crown. Most species tend to produce masses of shoots along the length of their trunks; rub these off while they are young and soft.

Special requirements: When mature, some species produce a rather dense crown and so pollarding can be practised. Pleaching is also an effective way to display a row of limes.

Trachelospermum
Star jasmine or Confederate jasmine

EVERGREEN CLIMBER

General: Sweetly scented jasmine-like flowers in summer and autumn, and glossy deep green, leathery leaves are the main features of this slightly tender twining shrub. Specimens tend to produce masses of shoots that, if left, become an unmanageable tangle. Thin out established plants during spring, keeping only enough shoots to clothe the wall.

Special requirements: In the first few years, you will need to guide some of the stems into position and tie them in.

Trachelospermum jasminoides

Ulex europaeus 'Flore Pleno'

Ulex
Gorse

LEAFLESS SHRUB

General: In spring, this spiny shrub of dense habit can be extremely dramatic with its yellow pea flowers. Prune after flowering, trimming back flowered shoots, removing dead wood and opening up the centre. Trim after later flower flushes to prevent seed formation.

Special requirements: Vigilance is required during dry weather as massed plantings of gorse will produce a large amount of dead wood and this can be a fire hazard.

Ulmus
Elm

DECIDUOUS TREE

General: The elm is one of the most stately and beautiful of large trees. Select a single leader and well-spaced laterals. Dutch elm disease has become widespread in the past century. With infected elms dead branches within the crown, and premature yellowing, are signs of trouble; if you lift some bark from the suspect branches and see insect galleries (the disease is spread by a beetle) this is a sure sign of the disease. Heavily infected trees must be removed and such an operation is best left to qualified fellers. Trees lightly infected will respond to having the infected branches lopped off: they should be removed and burnt without delay. Check remaining branches to ensure that there are no beetle galleries.

Special requirements: Even healthy elms can drop large limbs without warning, so do not allow branches to extend too far from the trunk.

Vaccinium
Blueberry and Billberry

see page 131

Viburnum

DECIDUOUS/EVERGREEN SHRUB

General: This is a large group of shrubs, popular for their rounded clusters of scented flowers (some blooming in winter), colourful autumn leaves and bright berries. Little pruning is necessary in general, but occasionally some of the oldest wood should be removed, and it may be desirable to trim some plants to shape following a heavy fruit set. Where pruning is deemed necessary, the winter flowerers are tackled during mid- to late spring; the summer flowerers in late winter and early spring, and the evergreens in mid-spring.

Special requirements: The evergreen *Viburnum tinus*, which has the common name of laurustinus, has a distinctive, dense habit. It responds well to hard pruning and will break freely from old wood.

Viburnum plicatum 'Summer Snowflake'

Vitis coignetiae

Weigela 'Eva Rathke'

Wisteria floribunda

Vitis Ornamental vine

DECIDUOUS CLIMBER

General: The pruning requirements of the hardy ornamental vines, the most common of which is *Vitis coignetiae*, are almost identical to those of the fruiting vines described on pages 132–3. The ornamental forms are grown mainly for their large, leathery leaves which turn to brilliant shades of red, yellow and purple in the autumn. If you are growing such vines over a tree, no pruning is required. If on a wall, fence or pergola however, where space is limited, after training in several rods all side shoots should be cut backing winter to one or two buds.
Special requirements: Do not delay pruning until the spring, otherwise the stems will bleed, possibly to the detriment of the plant.

Weigela

DECIDUOUS SHRUB

General: This hardy, deciduous shrub produces foxglove-like flowers in late spring and early summer. Flowering takes place on laterals from the previous year's wood. The pruning requirement is not great: ideally you should shorten or remove flowering stems immediately after the blooms have faded, during mid- to late summer. If a more drastic pruning is required, to keep the shrub within bounds or to remove some of the oldest wood, do this in early spring to allow the plant to produce a mass of new growth during the growing season.
Special requirements: Apart from its pink flowers, *Weigela* 'Looymansii Aurea' is also grown for its yellow leaves, and these are most dramatic on young wood; therefore, each year in late summer cut out a good proportion of old wood, to encourage plenty of new.

Wisteria

DECIDUOUS CLIMBER

General: Wisteria is a beautiful climber, and its late spring pendant flower clusters are some of the most highly scented of any garden plants. However, all too often wisterias are grown where there is insufficient space. All are vigorous, and if left alone their long stems and whippy shoots will dislodge slates, and block down pipes and gutters. After planting, cut all stems back by half, and continue to do this each spring until a well-spaced framework has been achieved. In mid-summer, cut back all young shoots to four or five buds, and in late winter cut back to two or three buds any further shoots that may have developed. This builds up a spur system, sò encouraging a greater number of flowers. It also has the effect of reducing extension growth. If training a Wisteria over a tree, no pruning is necessary.
Special requirements: A freestanding Wisteria can be produced. Train five leaders to a supporting stake, cutting them back to 1m (3ft) in the first winter; the next winter cut the new extension growth back to no more than 1m (3ft). Prune all side shoots, as already described in mid-summer and late winter.

Pruning Hardy Fruit Trees

The principles and practice of pruning are tested more with tree fruits than with ornamental garden plants. Flowering shrubs or hedges, for example, need to be shaped and restrained, but leaving them alone for a year or two, or giving them a few bad cuts in error, will not usually cause them lasting damage. Fruit trees are, however, less tolerant of the casual approach. To persuade them to produce good and regular cropping, from an early age, fruit trees should be 'built' into 'production units' and every piece of growth should have a purpose.

That said, there is a great deal of unnecessary mystery attached to their pruning. This has arisen partly because fruit growing has been around for millennia, and has accrued an enormous amount of folklore. Pruning is, actually, very often overdone. If there is any uncertainty on the part of the person doing the pruning, the tree is best left untouched; the projected cut abandoned. In other words, every act of cutting a piece of wood should have a reason.

Understanding Rootstocks

As most fruit trees will not breed true from seed or cuttings, the majority are budded or grafted onto rootstocks. Trees grown on

Pruning for health

One of the most important reasons for pruning fruit trees is often forgotten: the cure or avoidance of diseases.

Cankers: treat cankers of apples, cherries, pears and plums, under less severe circumstances, by cutting away the diseased tissues. With bad attacks it is easier to remove the complete branch. In either case a sharp knife should be used to cut away the damaged tissue, till you arrive at clean wood. Canker is often worse on trees in poorly drained soil.

Silver leaf: any fruit tree may suffer from this disease, but plums are particularly susceptible. It shows as silvering leaves, becoming brown in severe cases. Dieback of branches ensues and the whole tree may eventually be killed. All dead branches must be cut back to about 15cm (6in) behind the point where the stain in the inner tissues ceases.

Fireblight: the shoots of apples and certain ornamental trees become brown and withered, but do not fall. Cut out diseased wood to about 60cm (2ft) below the apparently affected tissues.

Peach leaf curl: this is troublesome on peaches, nectarines and almonds. The leaves develop reddish blisters. Spraying with a copper-based fungicide in winter is the best treatment, otherwise pinch out the infected shoots.

their own roots (that is, cuttings) and seedling trees are variable in size and vigour, and are slow to reach cropping age.

Rootstocks are chosen for their dwarfing effect, their resistance to certain pests and diseases, their fruiting capability and for a good root system. The tree's ultimate size and rate of growth are dependent on the rootstock, so it has a bearing on the training and initial pruning. The same cultivar of, say, apple may be available in two or more tree

Countless different varieties of apple, such as 'Lord Lambourne', have been bred and developed for centuries

Choosing the correct rootstock

FRUIT	ROOTSTOCK
Very dwarf (up to 1.8m/6ft high approx.)	
Apple	M27
Cherry	Tabel
Dwarf (up to 2.5–3m/8–10ft approx)	
Apple	M9
Pear	Quince C
Cherry	Gisela 5
Plum	Pixy
Gage	Pixy
Damson	Pixy
Peaches	Pixy
Semi dwarf (up to 3–4.5m/10–15ft high approx)	
Apple	M26
Cherry	Damil
Semi vigorous (up to 3.5–4.8m/12–16ft approx)	
Apple	MM106
Pear	Quince A
Plum	St Julien A
Gage	St Julien A
Damson	St Julien A
Peach	St Julien A
Nectarine	St Julien A
Apricot	St Julien A
Cherry	Colt
Vigorous (up to 4.5–6m/15–20ft high approx)	
Apples	MM111
Peaches	Brompton
Nectarine	Brompton
Plum	Brompton
Cherry	Inmil

Buying fruit trees

When buying fruit trees always look for plants that appear healthy, and with no visible signs of distress (wilting, yellowing or dull leaf colour). The containers should be clean and free from weeds. Ascertain that the rootstock used is suitable for its intended site and form. A vigorous tree, for example, can never be made or kept small by pruning; instead it will produce little or no fruit and masses of top-growth.

sizes if it is compatible with several different rootstocks.

Vigorous rootstocks produce large trees that need little pruning to crop year after year, whereas modern rootstocks produce smaller trees that need more careful tending. In some cases the rootstocks are given code numbers that refer to the place where they were developed: the 'M' series for apples originated at the East Malling horticultural research station in the English county of Kent. All rootstocks with the same code number will produce trees of near identical size. The more 'dwarfing' their effect, the quicker the tree will crop (see chart).

Family trees

A 'family tree' is an apple tree made up of several different cultivars growing on a single root system. Although it tends to have a high novelty value, it can serve to offer usually three different varieties from one tree, and this can be useful if space is at a premium.

A typical family tree – and which is currently commercially available – would comprise the dessert apple cultivars 'Discovery' (early), 'James Grieve' (mid-season) and 'Sunset' (late). Alternatively you could opt for a mix of dessert and culinary apples: 'Gala', 'Sunset' and the cooking apple 'Bountiful', for example.

Fruit Tree Shapes

Once you have grasped the idea of different rootstocks, it is easy to see that fruit trees can be fitted into almost any garden. For example, apples and pears in gardens where space is limited can be grown as dwarf bush, a larger bush, a cordon, a dwarf pyramid, a fan, an espalier, or even a single-stemmed columnar tree in the style of the 'Ballerina' and 'Minarette' strains available from some nurseries (see page 103).

The following are the most often-seen tree shapes:

Pyramid

Bush – an open-centred bush tree will have a main stem of about 60cm (2ft) with branches radiating outwards. A central-leader bush is where the main stem is continued vertically so that laterals arise over a greater length. Orchard managers often employ a variation of this, called the spindle bush, in which the lower branches of the tree are trained horizontally, for heavier cropping.

Standard and half-standard – a tree with a clear trunk of up to 2.1m (6½ft), and which is grown from the most vigorous rootstocks. In most gardens it is not practical to have this size of tree, so people tend to opt for half-standards with 1.05m (3½ft) of clear stem.

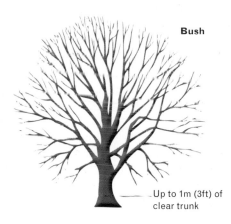

Bush

Up to 1m (3ft) of clear trunk

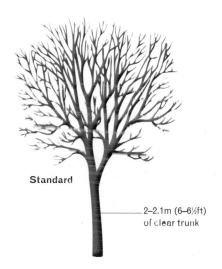

Standard

2–2.1m (6–6½ft) of clear trunk

Pyramid – this is a tapering tree, often reaching up to 2.5m (8ft) in height, with the lowest branches being the longest. It is used frequently with plum trees. The dwarf pyramid, reaching a maximum height of 2m (6ft) is perhaps best thought of as a free-growing vertical cordon (see below); good for apples and pears.

Fan – this is a form of training, against a wall or free-standing supports linked with wires, suitable for most tree fruits but particularly plums and peaches. The main stem of the tree to be trained is short, perhaps just 5–8cm (2–3in) in length, and the 'fan' of branches originates from two low, main branches.

Espalier (above); fan (above right); free-standing espalier in bloom in front of single-stemmed cordons against a wall (below)

Espalier – another form of training, suitable for apples and pears. The main stem extends vertically to the top-most wire, with branches trained horizontally and opposite along intermediate wires, giving the tree a formal symmetry. The lowest branches would be set along the lowest wires, leaving a clear stem of just 30cm (12in) or so.

Cordon – good for apples and pears, and also some soft fruits, a single-stemmed

cordon is trained against a wall or free-standing supports linked with wires. An oblique cordon (which is set at 45°) is very productive for its size and the amount of space it takes up. U-shaped and W-shaped (multiple) cordons may also be created, but these are generally grown upright rather than at an angle.

Training a Bush Tree

The most easily managed form of apple tree for today's average-sized garden is a bush tree, usually grown on M9 or M26 rootstocks. Open-centred bush trees are most commonly seen with about 60cm (2ft) of main stem, with leading branches radiating up and out.

The first three or four years are crucial in the life of an apple tree. There is a specific pruning operation required each year:

1 – Plant a maiden tree between late autumn and mid-winter, at the same time shortening it to about 68cm (27in), with the cut made just above a bud.
2 – A year later the tree will have formed healthy, strong primary branches. Select four that are coming out wide from the trunk.

2nd year: new growth and pruning cuts

3rd year: pruning of secondary branches

3rd year: pruning of central laterals

Remove all others at their points of origin, and cut back the four by about a half. Always cut to an outward-facing bud.

3 – After a further year, secondary branches will have formed. Again, cut back the leaders by about half, to outward-facing buds. At the same time any laterals growing towards the centre of the tree should be cut back to four buds to induce spurs. A well-spaced, open-centred bush tree is now becoming established.

This same basic training also applies to the pyramid, half- and full standard trees. The rootstock and cultivar type will determine the rates of growth and eventual sizes.

Training a Fan-Shaped Tree

A well-trained fan has a central stem and two short main arms, one on each side, from which ribs radiate outwards and upwards.

1 – Start by planting a young feathered tree with two strong, low laterals; ideally this should be in early spring. Tie these to angled bamboo canes to the wires, at around 45°.
2 – Cut back the leader to the higher of the two selected laterals, ideally to about 30cm (12in) from the ground. Then shorten the selected laterals, cutting to a downward facing bud, about 40cm (16in) or so from the trunk.
3 – Remove all other branches, but back to two buds. Do not remove these branches in their entirety, as the buds will produce leaves and so help to feed the tree during the growing season.
4 – During the first summer it is important to tie side shoots in regularly as they develop. Aim for an even spacing and development on each side of the fan, and make sure you retain low-growing shoots as well as those higher up the plant, otherwise the fan will not grow to its full potential. Each of the two arms should be allowed to extend.
5 – To establish the framework, over the next two years shorten the side shoots in the early spring to leave about 60cm (24in) of the previous year's growth.

Training Espalier Trees

ESPALIER
tie the angled laterals to the lowest
wire, to form the first tier

This form of training is really just a modified fan: a tree that consists of a central stem with horizontal branches coming out at intervals of about 37cm (15in).

1 – Plant an un-feathered maiden tree during early spring; it should be staked vertically in the soil. Then cut back the stem to 37cm (15in) from the ground.
2 – The uppermost bud will shoot out and become the new leader. This should be tied in to a vertical cane. The two buds lower down will become the bottom horizontal arms, and these should be tied, as they grow, at an angle of 45° to the main stem.
3 – The next autumn bring down the two side

Supporting framework for wire-trained fruits

Fan, espalier and cordon-trained trees require a supporting framework of posts and wire, which should be set up before the trees are planted. The posts must be sturdy, and remember that wooden posts will need renewing eventually.

Cordons Wires are best spaced at 60, 90, 120 and 150cm (2, 3, 4 and 5ft) from the ground. To support the actual plant, a bamboo cane, or something similar, must be secured to the wires at the required angle. Set the first tree approximately 1.8m (6ft) in from the end post, planting this and all subsequent trees at the same angle as the cane(s), with the scion part of the graft union in the uppermost position. This will prevent the union being forced open if the tree is bent lower when it reaches the top of the framework.

Fans Wires should be spaced at 15cm (6in) intervals. Trees should be planted centrally between the supporting posts, ensuring that there is enough room on either side of the main stem for the full length of the branches.

Espaliers Space the supporting wires at 45cm (18in) intervals and plant as for fans.

Multiple espaliered trees at commercial fruit farms are a common sight in some rural areas

branches to the horizontal support wires. Then cut back the vertical leader to within 45cm (18in) of the bottom branches, leaving three buds to continue the process all over again. Also, prune back the horizontal branches by about one third.
4 – With an established espalier tree, each year cut back the terminal growths on branches and central leader, to the junction with older wood. Thereafter undertake spur pruning.

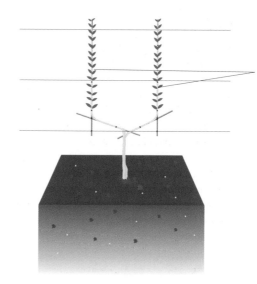

DOUBLE CORDON
prune the leader back to
two main buds, then tie
in the stems with angled
and vertical canes

SINGLE CORDON
train the leader at a 45° angle and
prune the laterals back close
to the main stem

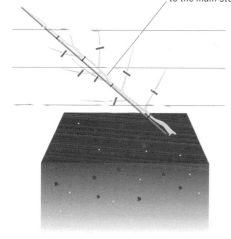

Training Cordons

The word 'cordon' usually refers to a single-
stemmed plant, but in fruit tree terms there
are also U-shaped and W (or multiple)
cordons. The plant stems can be trained
vertically or at an angle; 45° is recommended
because it receives maximum direct
sunlight. A single-stemmed cordon can be
created over a three-year period:

1 – Plant an unpruned maiden tree in spring,
tying it in several places to the pre-set
bamboo cane and/or support wires (see box
above). Do not tip or prune the leader, but
cut any side shoots back to four buds, the
aim being to create spur systems. No
further pruning is done for a full 12 months.

2 – In the meantime, the cut side shoots will
have produced sub-laterals and some of the
original buds will have transformed into
flower buds. A year after planting, any new
laterals should be pruned to four buds, and
the sub-laterals cut back to about 2.5cm
(1in) from their points of origin.

3 – A few apples may form in the second
summer but, to preserve the long-term
welfare of the tree, they should not be allowed
to ripen. Indeed, it is best to cut off flowers as
they appear in spring, but take great care to
leave the rosette of leaves intact.

4 – From now on, prune the laterals during
summer to check excessive vigour and
stimulate the formation of flower buds. Cut
back to three good leaves from the base, but
not counting the basal rosette. Again, cut
back the sub-laterals to about 2.5cm (1in).

5 – In the third winter, if summer pruning was
carried out the previous summer, cut the
laterals now to four buds, and the sub-
laterals back to 2.5cm (1in). Do not prune the
leader. If summer pruning had taken place,
this is still a good time to cut back any shoots
with flower buds to the outermost one. This
will cause the development of a fruiting spur.

6 – Finally, when the leader has passed the
top wire, cut away all of the one-year-old
wood back to its junction with the previous
year's growth.

Renovation Pruning

Old fruit trees are often found in a neglected state, and at first sight you might consider them fit only for digging up. However, with renovation pruning over a period of time, some trees can be given a new lease of life. In addition to the following recommended remedial action, you should cut out dead, diseased and damaged branches, as well as any that cross over others, causing the wood to rub against each other.

For neglected trees

If the tree has been neglected, rather than badly treated, it will be overgrown with much branched fruiting spur systems and a large amount of bare wood. A procedure known as de-horning should be carried out.

Cut out one or two branches each year, as close to the crotch of the tree as possible. Initially remove branches that crowd the centre, and later thin out the periphery if necessary. Aim to reduce overall height by cutting to a point where a lower branch can take over. Cut cleanly at these junctions.

If there are not many branches to be removed, but spur clusters are crowded on old wood, thin out these clusters by half, over a period of, say, four winters.

For 'hacked' trees

It may be that the tree has been 'hacked' instead of pruned, so that it has resulted in a mass of congested shoots, with little or no consequent fruiting. Here, whole branches need to be cut out before the shoots are thinned.
- Encourage a new framework of well-placed branches by selecting some of the best-placed shoots to be new leaders.
- Leave enough of the other shoots as laterals, which will carry fruit buds in time.
- Cut out the unwanted 'watershoots', which will be produced in profusion, unless pruning is spread over several seasons.

Is the tree worth saving?

Ask yourself these questions:

Is it a young tree? If so, chances are you will be able to make it usefully productive.
Is the tree in the right place and does it enhance the appearance of the garden? If yes, it may be worth spending the time and energy to improve it.
Does the tree take up too much room? If yes, then the overall garden may be improved by its removal.
Is there a significant amount of dead wood visible? If yes, then assess whether, once it has been removed, there will be enough remaining healthy tree to make it worth saving!

Thinning

It is natural for plants to increase in mass, but in the case of fruit trees such 'bulking out' can cause problems. Here are three instances where some judicial 'thinning' on the part of the gardener can help to increase the quantity and quality of fruits.

Spur thinning

In the case of neglected trees it is all too possible for spurs to develop in to clusters,

When spurs develop in to clusters, such as on this old apple tree branch, it is preferable to cut out the older, more complex spurs first

Half way through the thinning procedure and the branch is much less congested

The finished, spur-pruned branches

and for them to crowd each other, which is particularly noticeable when in leaf. The fruits do not have room to develop properly, and many fall prematurely as a result. Such spur clusters should be thinned out at pruning time:

- Aim to reduce the number by half over a four year period.
- Cut out older, more complex spurs first, followed by the weak or thin spurs.
- Remove spurs on the undersides of branches, too.
- Leave thick, healthy younger wood wherever possible.

Blossom thinning

Many fruit trees become prone to 'biennial bearing', which means that they crop heavily one year, and the following year they crop poorly. This may be due to frost damage, overfeeding, disease, or simply exhaustion after a heavy (or good) year. One way to counteract biennial bearing is to thin the blossoms. To break the cycle, in the spring of a suspected 'heavy year', remove nine out of every ten flower trusses. Pinch out the open flowers, or use scissors, but make sure you leave the rosette of leaves intact.

Fruit thinning

Some trees in certain years will naturally grow a mass of fruits in a single cluster. If they are allowed to develop, many will become deformed and drop early, leaving others that are small and poorly flavoured. It is also possible that the weight of several such clusters on a branch may be too much for it, causing it to snap.

Such clusters of fruits should be thinned out in early summer after the tree has dropped its infertile or deformed fruits:

Remove at least a half of such crowded clusters, cutting the fruits off by the stalks with secateurs.

Aim for about a 10–15cm (4–6in) space between dessert or eating apples, and 15–22cm (6–9in) between culinary or cooking apples. It may be necessary to repeat the operation in mid-summer.

Use stout or even pruning scissors to thin out overcrowded bunches of grapes.

When fruit is weighing down the parent plant, nip the fruit out using pruning scissors to thin out the crop

Apples

Malus sylvestris var. *domestica*

It is not hard to see why apples are the most widely grown of the tree fruits. One variety or another can usually be counted on to crop satisfactorily in most temperate countries and on most types of soil.

Many gardens possess gigantic old trees, but with the modern semi-dwarfing and dwarfing rootstocks there is now no need to

Regular, judicious pruning of apple trees will result in an abundance of lush, healthy fruit

grow large trees. Indeed, on dwarf trees regular jobs like picking, spraying and pruning can be done either from ground level or, at most, from a pair of step ladders.

With a little intelligent pruning, taking perhaps no more than 20 or 30 minutes per year, a tree will remain fruitful for 50 years or more. In the case of a dwarf apple, grafted on to, say, an M9 dwarfing rootstock, the average yield could well be more than 14kg (30lb) a year. Not a bad result for only half an hour's work!

Spur formation

We have already seen that apples grow from spurs, but what exactly are these woody structures? Essentially they are short branch systems carrying clusters of flower buds. The aim of apple (and pear) culture is to produce as many spurs as the tree can bear, remembering that each spur should produce fruit for a number of years. Fan,

TIP

Is it ripe?
The ultimate in apple pruning is the harvesting! An easy way to tell if the apple is ripe for picking is to gently hold the fruit and give it a slight twist. If it does not come away easily, without forcing it, then it is not ready.

espalier and cordon-trained trees are all spur bearing.

In many cases spurs will form naturally, but it is often necessary to induce them by the correct and specific procedure of pruning.

The following is how a fruiting spur can be created, over a four-year period:

1 – On, for example, a young tree, prune a lateral shoot back to about four buds from its base. Do this between late autumn and mid-winter. This will cause one or two shoots to grow from the buds nearest the cut. Usually the buds farthest from the cut will develop into rounder, plumper flower buds.

To create a fruiting spur, prune back a lateral shoot to about four buds

The buds furthest from the cut will end up producing rounder, plumper flower buds

2 – The following winter cut all wood away to leave the two or three flower buds.

3 – These will each produce an apple the following summer, behind which will be formed a new flower bud. A simple spur system has now been formed and the tree will become more productive, reaching optimum fruiting (with correct maintenance and pruning) within a couple of years.

Tip-bearing trees

Some varieties of apple, such as 'Bramley's Seedling', 'Blenheim Orange', 'Tydeman's Early' and 'Worcester Pearmain', are tip-bearers, which means that they produce the fruit buds on the tips of the previous year's shoots instead of on laterals or spurs. Although some tip-bearers respond reasonably well to spur pruning, most crop much more heavily if treated entirely differently.

The following is how a tip-bearer can be trained into production, over a four-year period (note that leader pruning will mean cutting out some of the fruit buds, but this should nevertheless happen until the

Abundant blossoms on a thoroughly pruned and well-shaped columnar apple tree

Columnar apple trees

In addition to the conventional fruit tree shapes discussed on pages 95–6, with apples there are also the columnar shapes made popular by nurseries in the 1980s and 90s. Referred to by the registered names of 'Ballerina' or 'Minarette', these slender, upright trees bear their fruits on short spurs along the length of the vertical stem. They are perfect for today's smaller gardens, because they can be planted as close as 1m (3ft) apart; they are also well-suited to growing in tubs on patios or balconies (as long as they are well secured and will not fall over during heavy wind). When mature, these trees are around 2.4–2.7m (8–9ft) in height, and for their bulk they are heavy croppers. They are also perfect for beginner gardeners, as they do not need any pruning! The down side is that there are only a limited number of cultivars available with these tree forms, so you may not be able to choose the type you like.

framework of the tree has been established):

1 – During the first year leave unpruned all strong laterals on the outer part of the tree. This will result in new extension growth, and flower buds will be formed on the oldest, or previous year's wood.

2 – During the second winter use secateurs to cut back the youngest lateral wood to the top-most flower bud, or to the junction with the old wood. Fruit will be carried on this pruned back lateral the following summer.

3 – During the third winter cut back the fruited lateral to leave a stub about 2.5cm (1in) long. This may seem drastic, but within 12 months a strong new lateral will be produced from this stub, which in turn is left unpruned, to start the renewal process all over again.

Pears *Pyrus communis*

Pears are juicy, sweet and delicious, but they are not always quite as easy to grow as apples. Some of the older stewing pears do well in colder climates, but the modern dessert varieties need warmth, and long summers are the best environment for success. Pears generally flower earlier in the season and thus are more susceptible to late spring frosts. If you live in a cold area, therefore, it is advisable to afford some form of protection to the pear tree, perhaps even to the extent that you grow it as a trained tree against a sunny fence or wall. Fruit spurs form more easily and abundantly on pears than on apples, so they are well suited to being trained in to shapes, such as cordon and espalier.

Historically pears were grown as standard trees on pear seedling stock; not surprisingly they made very large trees and

Ensuring pollination

Although there are some self-fertile pears, it is always a good idea to have another pear from the same pollination group (that is, flowering at the same time), nearby. Pears are effectively divided into three pollination groups, and the seasons tend to overlap slightly, so trees from adjoining groups may be able to pollinate each other.

When deciding on the varieties of pear to grow it is always best to seek advice from a specialist, or consult dedicated fruit books or catalogues, as some pears are self-sterile (meaning they will not pollinate other trees), and some others will not successfully pollinate trees within the same flowering groups.

Pears are harder to grow than apples, being more prone to disease and the vagaries of the climate. Prune them with care!

took years to come into bearing. These days smaller bush trees are grafted on to quince rootstocks, meaning that the trees will reach just 2.5–3.5m (8–12ft) in height and spread. They can start fruiting within two or three years of planting. This is a much better situation than we had 50 years ago: then pears were notorious for being slow to reach bearing age. Indeed, an old saying went: 'If you plant pears, you plant for your heirs!'

TIP

Is it ripe?
Fruits on a pear tree ripen quickly and, if they are not collected straight away, quickly deteriorate. Check the tree regularly (even daily during the picking season), but be careful not to bruise the delicate fruits. Pick the fruits directly the base colour starts to turn yellow, or pale off. Touch is not always a good guide, as a fruit that feels firm to the touch may be ripe and starting to rot from the inside.

Initial pruning

With pears it is generally easier to achieve a 'goblet' shape, with an open centre. To form a bush from a maiden tree, cut it back to about 75cm (30in) from soil level, straight after planting. Allow three well-spaced shoots to develop over the following growing season, then double the number of these by pruning each back by about one third the following winter. In the early years of the tree you will need to cut back some laterals by about half to encourage more growth, and to counteract the tendency for vigour to decline as fruiting begins.

The fortunate thing about pears is that, in the case of spur-fruiting cultivars, spurs will be formed naturally. If you prune the tree to form its shape, as described above, the spurs should develop of their own accord. Occasionally, with a tree that is slow to mature – say, no spurs developed within three years of planting – you may need to give it a hand. In this case, prune as for forming spurs on apples (see pages 102–3).

Tip-bearing cultivars 'Josephine de

Malines' and 'Jargonelle' need leader tipping until the framework of the tree is established.

Pruning established pears

Summer pruning is of more benefit to pears than apples, and is most important on trained forms. The method is to reduce weaker side shoots to four leaves and stronger ones to six leaves, and to do this in mid-summer. This should be followed in the winter, by pruning shoots back to two buds.

Leaders need to be cut back by a third in winter (with most apple varieties they are just tipped). Complicated spur clusters soon develop on pears and need to be thinned regularly to maintain fruit size.

Thinning In seasons when the fruit set is heavy, it may be advisable to do some hand thinning but not until after the fruitlets have definitely set and the tree has shed naturally its unwanted extras, which could well be more than half of the original fruit set. Snap the young fruits, when about 2.5cm (1in) across, from the stalks; try not to pull off the fruit stalk as the brittle fruit spur may be broken.

Pear trees are very susceptible to an unpleasant and deleterious condition named 'fire blight'

Medlar *Mespilus germanica*

This odd fruit is certainly not so popular today as it used to be, when every well-stocked kitchen garden seemed to have an aged tree. Today, medlars are frequently grown as much for their ornamental appearance as for their edible fruits, which can be eaten raw when over-ripe, but are more generally used in jellies and jams. People who have tasted such products made from medlars either enjoy or vehemently dislike them!

Medlars can be grown in any soil, provided the drainage is good. The leaves are dull and leathery, brightening in the autumn, and the self-fertile flowers are quite large. Growth is rather slow, making a round-headed, drooping tree.

Pruning It is most usual to grow them as a half-standard or full-standard tree. Little pruning is needed for standard trees after the preliminary training, which comprises the removal of all laterals back to two or three leaves during winter. When a tree reaches the height wanted, pinch out the leading shoot. Unless established trees are kept thinned out, a tangled mass of branches will result.

Harvesting The fruits should be left on the tree until the first sharp autumn frosts, and then picked off and kept in a cool place. They are best eaten when slightly over-ripe.

The bright fruits of the quince tree or bush have been used for centuries to make conserves

Quince *Cydonia oblonga*

In addition to their more common use as rootstocks for propagating pears, quinces are useful as a fruit, especially for making the familiar bright orange jelly. Or you might prefer quince jam, using the peeled and cored fruit. The quince is one of the oldest known fruits, often being referred to by Greek and Roman writers; some authorities even believe the quince to be the 'forbidden fruit' of the Garden of Eden rather than the apple.

Quinces, like pears, dislike cold winds and are not for planting in cold, exposed situations. However, in a mild district, and if given a fairly moist deep soil, quinces can be grown either as a bush or a half-standard tree.

Pruning Thin out overcrowded bushes during winter, to preserve an open-centred plant. To keep wall-trained trees within bounds, these can be cut back, at the same time, to two or three buds from the junction with the previous season's wood.

Harvesting The fruit does not ripen until mid-autumn, and it is best to leave the fruits on the plants for as long as possible, in order for the full characteristic flavour to develop. After picking, the fruits should not be stored close to either apples or pears as its strong aroma is liable to affect their flavour.

Medlars are not to everyone's taste and are best enjoyed when slightly over-ripe

Plums *Prunus domestica*

The plum family, which includes the gages, damsons, bullaces, cherry plums and Japanese plums (or Salines), are all generally heavy croppers. It is not uncommon to find a large, mature tree laden with perishable fruit, which usually tastes wonderful straight off the tree when ripe, but can just as usefully be used in all manner of desserts, puddings, jams and jellies.

Most forms of plum are self-fertile, but if there is a nearby variety in the same pollination group then you are more likely to get a bumper harvest. Flowers generally come early, often by mid-spring, which means that they are susceptible to frost damage. If you live in a cold area, therefore, you would be well advised to choose either a late flowering variety, or to grow a damson, which is hardier.

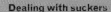

TIP

Dealing with suckers
Members of the plum family are prone to producing suckers, coming straight from the roots; some can be quite a distance from the trunk of the tree. They should be removed as soon as they are noticed, and preferably in the summer. Dig away the soil to expose the root and pull off the sucker. Do not cut it off as, no matter how close you get to the root, a small base with adventitious buds will be left, from which more suckers will arise. Any surface damage caused to the root by the pulling will soon heal.

'Victoria' is the most popular plum cultivar by far, whilst 'Czar', 'Rivers' and 'Marjorie's Seedling' follow closely. The plum strains known as gages are generally smaller and more rounded: the most popular are 'Denniston's Superb', 'Laxton's Gage' and 'Cambridge Gage'.

Plum pruning

In the first two or three years after planting plum trees tend to make a lot of strong wood growth, but after that they settle down to produce fruiting wood.

Correct pruning of plum trees must take place in the early stages of their growth, before they become too established:

1 – Cut back a maiden tree in spring to about 90cm (3ft). Shorten the feathers to 5–8cm (2–3in).
2 – Next winter choose four evenly spaced shoots at the top of the main stem and cut them back by half.
3 – The following year cut back by half the new growth from these. Always cut back to outward facing buds. Also remove overcrowding and crossing branches.

An established plum tree need only be pruned regularly if it is necessary to restrict its growth, and this should be done in late spring when it is in active growth (to avoid infection by silver leaf disease).

A healthy plum tree will produce abundant fruit, but these plants do suffer from pests and diseases, especially silver leaf

There are many different varieties of plum, some good eaten raw, others better for cooking

Fruit thinning

The plum more than any other fruit responds to sensible thinning; do not do the entire thinning in one go, however, spread it instead over several days to reduce the shock to the plant. The best time to thin is when the fruit has finished stoning (which you can tell by selecting a single fruit and slicing it open, and looking to see if there is a small brown stone in the centre). All diseased, bruised or misshapen fruits should first be removed. Snap the stalk on the shoot; do not pull off the stalk as this may injure the shoot and next year's crop.

Harvesting

Commercial growers of plums usually clear their trees in one go, but the amateur has the benefit of picking over the crop and selecting only the suitable fruits. Gages, in particular, ripen unevenly, needing two or three pickings to allow full flavour to develop. Most fruits should part readily from the stalk, but sometimes damsons can be tricky to remove. Take care not to damage the spur.

Plums should not be picked when they are wet, as their natural wax can be damaged and this can assist brown rot infection. Whilst picking, clear the tree of any rotting or damaged plums, as this will help to prevent fungal diseases.

Damsons

Both the blue-black coloured damsons, and the closely related bullaces, which are smallish plum-like fruits, ripen in the autumn. The true damson has a unique flavour and is highly regarded on that account for jam making.

The 'Merryweather' damson is often purchased and grown, the gardener believing that a damson is a damson! However, this form is more like a plum, as not only does it lack the real blue-black colour, but also its skin is thicker and the flesh is a greenish yellow, and lacks the full damson flavour; it is, however, a heavy cropper. Two other popular damsons are 'Shropshire Damson' and 'Bradley's King'.

Damsons can live to great ages and more often than not someone who takes over an old tree will find that the pruning requirement is to renovate thoroughly rather than maintain a healthy cropping tree. If this is the case, cut out a few of the main branches of the tree completely to create a well-spaced framework. Thin out the side shoots, as well. New shoots will then develop, which can rejuvenate the framework. All pruning is best done in the summer, and can be spread over two years. Healthy trees should be treated as for plums.

Cherries *Prunus* spp.

There are both sweet (also known as dessert) cherries, and acid (also known as sour or 'Morello') cherries, and just to be confusing there are also 'Duke' cherries, which are a hybrid between the two. The main distinguishing feature is the difference in size of the tree: sweet and 'Duke' traditionally being large, whilst 'Morello' trees grow to little more than 3.6m (12ft) in height. All cherries can be grown well against a wall, provided there is enough space.

Cherries are more exacting than most fruit trees as far as soil conditions are concerned; good drainage is essential; a deep loam overlying chalk would be ideal. The trees blossom early, so districts subject to spring frosts and cold winds are less

> **Selecting rootstocks**
> Cherries on their own rootstocks grow very large; however the Colt and Inmil semi-dwarfing rootstocks make them much more suited to the average sized garden. The vigour of Colt is roughly comparable with that of MM106 apple rootstock. Inmil, a rootstock developed in Belgium, is sometimes listed as rootstock GM19.

TIP

suitable unless some protection can be afforded. Warm conditions during the growing season produces the finest cherries. The best planting time is late autumn.

It is wise to go carefully with fertilizers high in nitrogen on these plants, as otherwise wood growth could be excessive, but for good results potash and phosphates will be needed.

Pruning cherries

Pruning and training should only be carried out during the growing season when the risk of silver leaf and bacterial canker gaining entry to the wood is at the lowest level.

Sweet cherries

Sweet cherries (*Prunus avium*) may be grown as either bush tree or fan-trained. Several varieties are available, the best known being 'Merton Glory', 'Early Rivers', 'Stella' and 'Sunburst'. Prune established sweet cherries as little as possible. If you need to keep the tree within bounds, cut side shoots back to five or six leaves from the base in mid-summer then shorten these again during autumn to three or four leaves.

Old-time gardeners used to say that sweet cherries should be pruned at planting time and never again. Methodology has changed over the years, but it does rather suggest that pruning is not vital to these plants; it merely improves shape and efficiency.

Acid cherries

Fruits of the acid or 'Morello' cherry (*Prunus cerasus*) are ready for picking from mid- to late summer. It can be grown either as a fan or an ordinary tree. If the latter, the pruning

Both sweet and acid cherries are more exacting over growing conditions, but sweet cherries, in particular, do not need too much in the way of pruning

However strong your desire to grow cherries, the first question you should ask yourself is whether you can protect the ripening fruits against marauding birds. Without the possibility of complete protection against many of our frequent garden birds, blackbirds and starlings in particular, it is a waste of time contemplating the planting of either sweet or acid cherries. For this reason it is easier to grow trained trees on a fence or wall, that can be entirely netted.

It is essential to harvest your cherry crop as soon as possible after the fruits have ripened

Training as bush trees

To form a bush tree of either a sweet or acid cherry:

1 – Cut back a maiden whip to about 75cm (30in) tall; this should be carried out in early spring, as growth is beginning.
2 – A year later, select three or four of the best-placed shoots and cut out all the rest. The retained shoots should be at a wide angle to the stem to make a strong joint. If enough shoots are present, it is often wise to remove the top one; it is normally too upright and vigorous for best results. Cut back the retained shoots, to outward pointing buds, to leave about 45cm (18in) of stem.
3 – By the following year there will be a good head of up to 10 strong, young branches. Again, prune these back to 45cm (18in); it is unlikely that any more leader pruning will be needed. The first crops should appear in the following year.

consists of cutting older shoots back to one-year-old laterals in spring, after the buds have burst. Fruit is only produced on the previous year's wood, so aim at getting a constant supply of vigorous new growth.

Fan-trained trees should be pruned in much the same way, once the basic framework of the fan is established. In addition, you will need regularly to rub out buds growing on the side of the tree facing the wall.

Cherries are one of the most attractive and versatile of all summer fruits, but unfortunately birds love them, too!

Training as fan-trained trees

Although two-year and sometimes even four-year-old trees are often recommended, it is arguably better to buy a one-year-old tree and train it yourself; if you do buy an older tree it should already be fan-trained.

The aim should always be to keep the central part of the fan open until the side branches are well established, as those in the middle always grow vigorously and will soon catch up. Follow the general advice for training fans (see page 97).

Peaches, Nectarines & Apricots

Prunus persica, P. armeniaca

The difference between peaches and nectarines – both *Prunus persica* – concerns skin texture only: peaches have a furry skin and nectarines have a smooth one. The growing and pruning techniques are identical, although nectarines are slightly more tender, requiring a sheltered site if it is to grow successfully outdoors in cooler climates. The apricot (*P. armeniaca*) looks similar, but produces smaller fruits with a more tart flavour. Apricots seem, also, to be more tender.

Because the flowers of all three open in early spring, frost protection is necessary for trees growing outside. Then, after fruit set, warm and sunny conditions are required for complete success through to the ripened fruits. An unheated greenhouse goes a long way to help; here trees growing in large containers are most appropriate, unless you have a very tall, lean-to type greenhouse with a good soil run. Outside, a warm, sunny wall gives protection and some extra warmth, which makes all the difference, but the soil in such a place can be very dry so watering during the growing season is often necessary.

Free-standing trees are more difficult to look after, so fan-trained types are best. These can be purchased as two- or three-year-old trees, trained initially in the nursery. Mid- to late autumn is the best planting time and a well-drained soil is essential.

These fruits require a little extra lime in the soil, not only for general health but also for stone formation within the fruits.

Nectarines share the same botanical name and many characteristics of peaches, but have a smooth skin

Peaches are hardier than nectarines and have rougher, slightly hairy skins

Choosing varieties

Peaches 'Peregrine', 'Rochester' and the 'Duke of York' are the most popular varieties grown by the home gardener, but there are many more.

Nectarines A nectarine is the smooth-skinned mutant, or sport, of the peach. 'Early Rivers' and 'Lord Napier' are the two most popular varieties, cropping during mid-summer.

Apricots There are fewer varieties of apricot available to the amateur, but there is always reliability with the forms 'Moorpark' and 'Alfred'.

Pruning requirements

Peaches produce fruit on the previous year's wood. Pruning, therefore, entails cutting out fruited shoots so that they are replaced with new stems to fruit the following year:

1 – As buds burst in spring, choose two towards the base of the previous year's growth. These will develop into the fruiting shoots for next year. Rub out any buds below the chosen two.

2 – The terminal bud on each shoot should be allowed to grow, but when it has produced about six leaves, pinch it back to four.

3 – Tie in and thin the fruits to about 23cm (9in) apart. Shoots where the fruits are being allowed to remain should be pinched back to two leaves from the older wood.

Nectarines In the same way as peaches, the fruits are carried on shoots that are produced the previous season. Because nectarines flower early it is the blossom, rather than the plant, which is tender. This must therefore be protected. Prune as for peaches.

Apricots This is not an easy fruit to grow, and if it fails to thrive this can be more to do with the soil or other growing conditions rather than the pruning. Dieback (dead shoot tips) can be common, and cutting to a healthy bud can control this.

In cooler climates, outdoor apricots are generally fan-trained against a warm wall, because the flowers, which start opening in late winter, can quickly be killed by late frosts. Pollinating the flowers by hand is always an aid with apricots because they are self-fertile.

1 – Trees fruit mainly on the previous year's growth, so remove fruited shoots and replace with new shoots which will fruit the following year, as for peaches.

2 – Spurs of older wood also carry fruit, so these should be encouraged.

3 – Fruiting laterals do not stay particularly productive and should be cut out after three or four years, with new replacement shoots encouraged.

Thinning

Fruit thinning is almost always needed on peaches and nectarines (provided that pollination was adequate). A healthy tree should be able to carry a fruit every 23cm (9in) or so of fruiting shoot. So, a shoot 30cm (12in) long should support one fruit, whilst one 50cm (20in) long will support two. Thinning should take place when the fruitlets are a centimetre or so across. Remove first any that are diseased, damaged, misshapen, trapped behind a wire or branch, or that are particularly small. A second thinning may be required when the fruits are 2.5cm (1in) across.

In order to thrive, apricots rely upon the correct climatic and soil conditions rather than regular pruning

Figs *Ficus carica*

This succulent fruit, often grown for its foliage decoration alone, crops best if given the shelter of a warm wall. Coming from the Mediterranean region, it grows best in a sunny spot with a dryish soil. The varieties 'Brown Turkey' and 'Brunswick' are the most often seen forms growing in gardens, but there are many others available, with varying degrees of appeal.

Pruning requirements

Growing it as a fan against the wall is an excellent idea. A fully-grown fan-trained fig can occupy about 3.6m (12ft) length of wall. Although larger trees can be grown, they tend to become bare at the base and much of the wood is unproductive. A good tree size to aim for is one with five or six main branches.

Pruning is simple:
1 – During the early part of the growing season, stop all new growths as soon as they have produced five or six leaves. This will encourage more shoots to form and reduces the number of unwanted embryo fruits
2 – At the same time cut back last year's fruiting stems to one or two buds.
3 – Also prune away any winter-damaged wood, suckers and some thinning of wood may be appreciated.

Fruit oddities

Rather oddly, the fruits form one year, overwinter on the trees, and then ripen in the following summer. The situation is made stranger by the fact that the embryo figs appear in the axils of the leaves and are produced more or less continuously throughout the growing season, and not just in the spring as with most other fruits.

Thinning

Only those fig fruitlets that form towards the end of the growing season should be kept. Those appearing earlier in the year should be removed as they are too small to develop and ripen during the current season, and will be too large to withstand the cold of winter. Remove any new fruits that appear until late summer, so that only one or two embryo fruits remain on the end of each shoot at the onset of winter.

TIP

Restricting roots
Established plants benefit from root pruning every couple of years (see page 34). But a way around this would be to containerize the plant, perhaps in a large wooden tub, which is sunk into the soil. Indeed, as figs are grown from cuttings – and not grafted like most other tree fruits – a dwarfing effect can be achieved by keeping the root system small. If growing in open ground, try planting it in a pit lined by bricks (or concrete), just 60cm (2ft) or so square. Cover the bottom of the pit with broken crocks to provide good drainage.

If you opt to grow a fig tree in a large pot, tub or urn, then you will have the benefit of being able to move it to a sheltered position for winter protection. In this case, you should not allow the trunk to get longer than 60cm (2ft), simply for ease of transportation.

Fig trees need plenty of warm sunlight and careful pruning in order to do well. They are not naturally suited to northern climes

Mulberry *Morus nigra*

The nursery rhyme behoves us to go around the 'mulberry bush', but in fact mulberries can grow to large trees some 7.5m (30ft) in height at maturity. There are two forms: the black mulberry (*Morus nigra*) and the white mulberry (*M. alba*). The former is grown for its berries, which appear in late summer. They are not as you would image a tree's fruits to be: they look very much like loganberries – very dark red when fully ripe. They are also, like the loganberry, better in cooking than eaten raw. The white mulberry provides the leaves for feeding silkworms. Both forms make fine ornamental trees.

Pruning requirements

Mulberries are frequently identified by their low-growing habit and oddly shaped branches, often in need of propping up. This can look rather endearing, but it is not ideal, and so a standard tree is the best form to buy and maintain, because the branches are high off the ground. It will take many years for them to develop the natural weeping habit.

Mulberries fruit on the current season's shoots as well as on spurs borne on older wood. Pruning mature trees is not to be encouraged as they bleed sap whenever cut, so it should really be limited to shaping the tree in its early years. Any remedial pruning of older trees should be carried out in early winter.

Mulberry fruits resemble a cross between a raspberry and a blackberry

Persimmon is an unusual-looking fruit that requires very warm weather to be at its best

Japanese Persimmon *Diospyros kaki*

This fruit, which comes from the Far East and is grown commercially in many hot countries, really does need warm weather to thrive. It makes an attractive, round-headed plant, with very beautiful autumn colour in the leaves, in colours from yellow through to red and purple. The fruit, which grows to 7.5cm (3in) across, is in the form of a fleshy berry, green at first then becoming yellow, orange, brown and then purple just as autumn comes to a close.

Pruning requirements

Fruits are carried on current season's wood. Trees are usually trained with a clear trunk of some 60cm (2ft). Good formative training is necessary as the wood can be brittle, and may snap under the weight of a heavy crop. Remove all weak branches. It can take up to five years to develop a good framework of branches.

Pruning established plants is not necessary. If you need to make cuts do this in winter. Thin the centre of overcrowded trees to promote good air circulation, and remove any dead, diseased or damaged wood.

Pruning Exotic &
Tender Fruits
& Nuts

If you have a reasonably sized greenhouse, conservatory or even sun room as part of your home, and you fancy trying to grow some of the more exotic types of fruits – the sorts that are frequently found for sale in supermarkets, but which you have never before seen actually growing on plants – then this chapter will be of interest to you.

We start off with the largest family of tender fruits: the citrus. Apart from oranges and their close relations the Satsuma, Clementine, Tangor and Tangelo (collectively known as 'mandarins') there are of course lemons, limes and grapefruits. All can be grown at home in cooler, temperate climes, provided they are afforded varying degrees of protection.

Less common exotic fruits, like the star fruit, paw-paw, breadfruit, lychee and custard apple, do require a bit of research to discover their optimum growing conditions,

and this makes it even more satisfying when you make a success of growing them.

This chapter concludes with nut trees. Some, like the hazel and walnut, are hardy, but it makes sense to include them here with their more tender cousins: the cashew, pecan, macadamia, pistachio and brazil nuts.

As long as you have the space, and the desire, to grow the tender fruiting plants discussed in this chapter, the cultivation requirements of weather protection, heating and humidity, are relatively minor points!

Citrus *Citrus* spp.

The thrill of seeing ripe fruits on a home-grown citrus tree at Christmas time takes some beating! The perfume of citrus blossom can fill a conservatory or greenhouse in season, the fragrance perhaps reminding you of magical holidays abroad, memories filled with images of large trees in groves, laden with magnificent orange or yellow fruits.

In most cases citrus trees can be planted in containers, but they will need an acid

Nuts are among the more exotic fruits that it is possible to grow at home if you have a greenhouse or conservatory

compost, as well as the right food. In summer, citrus can be placed outside. The trees do not go dormant in winter and in fact are very productive, so they will need nutritional support at this time.

Types to grow

All citrus make good conservatory plants, and can be raised from pips as fun plants. For the best fruits, however, named cultivars should be grown. These are available from specialist fruit nurseries.

Lime (*Citrus aurantiifolia*) Small tree, 5m (16ft) in the wild, smaller in pots. Fruits have a thick green-yellow skin and pale green flesh. Very acid.

Seville orange (*C. aurantium*) The hardiest citrus, the fruits of which are used for making marmalade. Tree grows to 10m (33ft) in the wild; not suited to container growing. Fruits are round, deep orange. Sour.

Lemon (*C. limon*) Large shrub or small tree up to 6m (20ft) in the wild. Good for container growing. Oval, thin-skinned green fruits, maturing to bright yellow. Acid.

Meyer's lemon (*C. x meyeri* 'Meyer') A lemon-orange hybrid; similar to the lemon in all respects, except that the fruits are pale orange. Good pot plant. Acid.

Grapefruit (*C. x paradisi*) Large tree to 15m (50ft), not suitable for pot culture. Large, round fruits of pale yellow, sometimes pink. Sweet/sour.

Mandarin, Satsuma, Tangor (*C. x nobilis*) Small trees to 8m (26ft), good for growing in pots. The fruits are round, slightly flattened and have thin rind; usually orange-red. Sweet.

Sweet orange (*C. sinensis*) The most common form of citrus. Trees can grow to

Meyer's lemon, *Citrus* x *meyeri* 'Meyer' is an unusual lemon-orange hybrid featuring pale orangey-green fruits

TIP As a protection against the hot sun, and any winter frost, the citrus produces most of its fruit in the centre of the plant, hidden amongst the leaves and branches. Therefore, you should not be too hasty in removing the centre growth.

12m (40ft), but there are many smaller forms that make good container plants. Fruits are round and orange. Sweet.

Tangelo (*C. x tangelo*) A hybrid citrus with both *C. x nobilis* and *C. x paradisi* in its parentage. Can grow to 8m (26ft), and makes a good container plant. Fruits are similar to Mandarin. Sweet.

Pruning requirements

Citrus trees can be pruned to a desired shape and size at any time, however it is best to prune immediately after fruiting and before new growth starts to appear (mid-winter is ideal). This encourages the tree to produce new growths within the area you

Sooty mould afflicts the leaves of citrus plants and is a relatively common problem. Prune away as necessary

Rootstock As with all woody fruiting plants that are grafted, remove any shoots that sprout below the graft as you do not want to encourage the rootstock to take over. The rootstock itself is invariably another form of citrus, most likely man-made hybrids known as 'Troyer' or 'Carrizo'. Lemons are not compatible with 'Carrizo', so they will always be grown on either 'Troyer' or the older sour-orange rootstock.

Watershoots In spring, citrus trees may produce one or two very vigorous new shoots (watershoots) that seem to be out of proportion to all the others, and often with bigger leaves. This is quite normal and it is not necessary to remove these growths, as the tree will eventually fill out. However, if you feel that these growths do in fact spoil the appearance of the tree, the shoots can be cut back to a more agreeable size, or trained to become sturdy branches using loose ties to hold them in the exact position you desire.

Citrus trees produce a branch from each leaf node, so watch out for this when pruning

require. With certain forms, which fruit continuously, this may mean sacrificing some blossom or fruit that may be present at the time of pruning.

Citrus trees will produce a branch from each leaf node, so take this into account when pruning, making sure that you are always producing a plant of good shape. Cut back to a leaf node that is pointing in the direction you would like to see new growth take. Fruit is produced on old and new wood, and even a quite mature, bare branch can sprout new growth. If a mature tree is looking tired, and not cropping too well, a hard pruning may help improve its vigour; but be aware that, in some cases, a good dose of fertilizer may be all that is necessary.

It is always preferable to prune your tree annually, or pinch out the tips of new growth when it reaches the desired length, as this will produce better-shaped trees. If you leave it too long before you prune, the branches of the tree may become thick, the pruning will be more difficult and the results could be patchy.

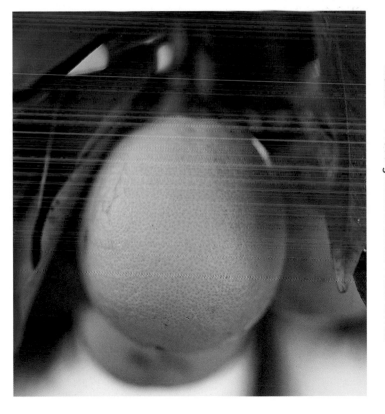

Custard Apple
Annona reticulata

The custard apple is an odd-looking fruit that originates from South America

In its native sub-tropical and tropical America this tree can grow to over 9m (30ft), but as it requires frost-free conditions in temperate countries it should be grown under glass, preferably in a large container. The fruits are some 10cm (4in) across, round and ripening red-green, with a yellow flesh. The soil within the container, (or glasshouse border), should be a fertile loam mixed with leafmould; good drainage is essential.

Pruning requirements Prune for a well-spaced framework of branches, and to keep the plant compact. You will need to keep the plant small, and fruit production may therefore be limited to just a few fruits per year.

Breadfruit
Artocarpus altilis

This plant (the seeded form of which is known as the breadnut) comes from the region around Malaysia, and has been cultivated for centuries. It is used as a vegetable boiled, baked or ground in to flour for biscuits; the roasted seeds are reminiscent of chestnuts. Being a tropical plant it is only with greenhouse cover that you can grow it in cooler countries. A minimum night winter temperature of 15°C (55°F) is required. Under such conditions it is unlikely that a plant under six years of age will bear fruit.

Papaya or Paw-paw
Carica papaya

A native of South America, this vitamin-rich fruit with deep yellow or salmon-coloured flesh has a firm, creamy texture and a delightful flavour reminiscent of melon and apricot. It needs a fertile, well-drained soil –

a waterlogged soil can kill it within days. Due to their susceptibility to wind scorch they should be grown only in sheltered conditions. It is perhaps best to grow papaya in a large, well-crocked pot, kept in a greenhouse or conservatory, in full sun, with a minimum winter temperature of 18°C (60°F).

Fruits are best ripened on the tree and are thus usually sweeter; they can also be picked when semi-ripe, and stored at 10°C (50°F) for two to three weeks. Unripe fruits can be cooked as for squashes, used in preserves or fermented into a kind of sauerkraut. Ripe fruits make a great dessert or breakfast fruit. It makes an unusual foliage plant, with dark green, deeply lobed leaves. The plants are short-lived and should be replaced every four years or so.

Pruning requirements The fruit is borne directly on the trunk, in the leaf axils, and plants are commonly grown and fruited as a single stem, although it is possible to encourage side shoots by pruning the tips when the plant is young. Thin the fruits to ensure that they grow to a good size, and to reduce pest damage (fruit clusters provide cover for insects).

Papayas, also known as paw-paws, are susceptible to pest problems which can be alleviated by pruning

Pomegranate

Punica granatum

This tender shrub – which can be grown outside in mild parts, preferably against a sunny wall – has particularly attractive flowers. The fruit may ripen in such a position, but to be sure of fruiting you should grow it under glass.

Pruning requirements It may be trained up to the support or grown as a bush. The latter method is the better one, although it will have considerable spread, perhaps 2.4m (8ft) from the wall, and is also low-branching. When trained up close to a wall the main branches are tied in to a fan. Growths coming away from the wall should be cut back as the buds break in the spring.

It responds well to pruning, and some of the older and weaker wood may be cut out during the spring or early summer. Wood should not be cut out during the winter as it is then difficult to distinguish living from dead. In severe winters Punica may be cut back into the old wood, which, if alive, will break out strongly.

Star Fruit

Averrhoa carambola

A native of the Asian tropics, this is grown primarily for its fruit which, with a mature tree in its natural habitat, may be harvested two or three times a year. The fruits, which are a common sight now in supermarkets, are golden yellow with three to five characteristic longitudinal ribs. They have a quince-like aroma when ripe. In favourable conditions flowers and fruit are borne almost continuously.

The tree is upright, symmetrical and low branching, ever so slightly frost hardy. Young forms will suffer some damage at temperatures just above freezing point, although older specimens of this plant can be more tolerant.

Pomegranates need to be grown in plenty of warm sunshine for the fruits to succeed

Grow loquats as free-standing trees and thin with judicious pruning

Star fruits are only just frost hardy, so offer some protection in the winter

Loquat

Eriobotrya japonica

The loquat, which has attractive, large, dark green leaves, is too large to train against a wall or fence, so it is usually grown as a freestanding small tree. As flowering takes place in the autumn, and the fruit does not ripen until the following summer, few fruits tend to survive the winter.

Pruning requirements Pruning consists of removing any blackened foliage, and thinning in mid-spring. It is possible to grow it against a large, high wall: either retain a lead to form a trunk, and loosely secure the main branches and stem to the wall; or, in a more restricted space, encourage branching from near ground level.

In milder parts the plant may be allowed to grow away from the wall, when the branches will spread out perhaps as far as 2m (6ft).

Lychee

Litchi chinensis

In sub-tropical parts of the world, this native of China is grown for its fruit, rich in vitamin C. The flesh is succulent and white, and may be eaten fresh or dried and preserved in syrup. The tree is attractive, round-topped and evergreen; slow to mature, but long-lived. The leaves are copper-red when young The fruits have rose-red outer casings, and are harvested in bunches, about 100 days after blooming. Fruit should be fully mature when picked, as it will not ripen once removed from the tree. Plants need to be kept frost-free all year round.

Pruning requirements Prune young trees only to establish a well-spaced framework. Heavy pruning, followed by an application of fertilizer, may rejuvenate older specimens. Nicking, notching or scoring branches in autumn is sometimes practised to induce heavier flowering the following spring.

Mango

Mangifera indica

Mango fruits are the most widely eaten fresh fruit in the world. They have been known to exist for more than 4000 years and there are over a thousand different varieties. The plant originated in south-east Asia, but is now grown in frost-free places around the globe. And this is the crucial point: Mangifera will not tolerate freezing temperatures.

The fruit develops from flower to maturity over a period of five months, and the fruits themselves are kidney shaped. They are an excellent source of vitamins A and C, but do not eat the skin of the fruit, as this can cause irritation of the mouth.

The trees are dome-shaped, evergreen and can grow to 18m (60ft) tall. They are often grafted for farming, but will fruit from seed after four to six years. As tropical fruits, they require hot, dry periods to set fruit and produce a good crop.

Pruning requirements Ideal for a conservatory or greenhouse, once trees have reached fruiting age they will need to be pruned annually to keep them under control. Prune back after harvesting, to outward facing buds, to encourage strong new shoots that will then bear fruit the following year. At the same time, remove any wood that is dead, damaged or diseased.

Mango is a sweet and extremely popular fruit that has been cultivated for thousands of years

Olive

Olea europaea

This is a tender tree, needing a sheltered, sunny garden in a mild area to succeed. Even so, after severe winters there may be considerable die-back and dead wood.

Pruning requirements When freestanding it is usually trained to a single leader; side shoots are shortened and retained as long as possible. Some thinning may be necessary. In less favoured gardens it is trained against a wall for protection, either tiered or fanwise. In mid-spring cut back shoots coming away from the wall, thin out growth, and trim to shape.

Generally six to eight main branches are trained fan-wise, with additional laterals tied in as they develop. The growths, which develop from this system, must be restricted and thinned by careful pruning. Promising shoots may also be used as replacements for any older branches that show signs of failing. In terms of visual appeal, young growths are always the most attractive parts of this plant.

With age, large, woody stems and branches develop, and the shrub may become unsightly. The remedy for this is to cut the whole tree back down to the ground level, in spring so that a fresh start may be made with the young growths that break out freely.

Avocado

Persea spp.

Many people try to grow avocado plants from the 'stone', but then throw the plant away when it gets too lanky and fails to produce any fruits. In fact, such plants can flower and fruit – but only after eight years or so – and it is perfectly possible to keep a good shape with careful pruning.

Some avocados are hardy, and will tolerate short periods of freezing, which gives many people the option of planting them out in the garden, especially in sheltered city or

Try planting up to three avocado varieties together in the same large-size pot and keep them together for life. This increases the chance of pollination. You could even choose to graft more than one variety onto a rootstock, as a 'family tree'.

maritime gardens. Leaves usually remain on the tree for up to three years.

Pruning requirements To keep established trees in containers to a size you can cope with, pinch out the growing tips. Remove dead, diseased and damaged wood, and any that is crossing or rubbing other wood. All pruning should be carried out after fruiting.

Cashew
Anacardium occidentale

Originally from the American tropics, the cashew has become widely distributed through cultivation. In addition to the well-known nut, its swollen receptacle, the cashew apple, is also edible and is used in jams and jellies. The shell of cashews is poisonous, but is destroyed on roasting. The plants crop from four or five years of age, requiring little in the way of aftercare. In temperate countries it can only survive under glass.

Pruning requirements Try to develop an open-centred tree, with a clear trunk of 1m (3ft) or so. Aim for four or five main branches, and tip this back each year to encourage more laterals. Established trees have no specific pruning requirements, other than to remove dead, damaged and diseased wood, and to keep the tree free from overcrowding.

Brazil
Bertholettia excelsa

The Brazil nut tree occurs naturally in deep rich alluvial soils around the Amazon basin.

It is one of the tallest trees of the region, up to 40m (130ft) tall, with a characteristically long straight trunk, branching only at the top. The fruits are large and spherical, with a hard woody casing, not unlike a coconut. Inside the shell are 12–24 brazil nuts packed like the segments of an orange. They take over a year to mature, and drop when ripe – sometimes from a great height, and as the entire fruit can weigh almost 2kg (4½lb). Being a collector can be a hazardous profession!

In temperate countries Bertholettia will only survive under hothouse glass conditions and will not set fruit.

Pruning requirements Keep it as a small plant, pruning during winter. Young trees can be induced to produce branches low down, by pruning back the main leader and shortening the main framework branches.

Pecan
Carya illinoinensis

The pecan is not an easy plant to grow away from its natural habitat and conditions. It never thrives in cooler climates, mainly because there is insufficient sun to ripen the wood properly. It is thus prone to coral spot and other destructive organisms. To produce crops, the pecan needs a dryish, warm climate with a hot summer and a cold but frost-free winter.

All species are fast growing and will normally form good straight leaders, developing into fine, shapely trees. It is important that they grow without any check.

Pruning requirements As the lead and upper branching extends, form a clear trunk of at least 2m (6ft), choosing autumn to mid-winter as the pruning period (trees bleed sap at other times). Usually, with a straight trunk and leader, lateral branching is not extensive. Leave the lower and outer branches to grow down to eye level; with a dark background to the autumn colouring, the effect is very pleasing.

Brazil nuts need tender loving care and will not grow outside in temperate climates

Cashews are tasty and popular but very hard to grow except under glass

Sweet chestnut
Castanea sativa

This tree produces those familiar, edible conker-like nuts, but in many colder areas it can be difficult for the nuts to reach sufficient size.

Pruning requirements Grow as a freestanding tree with a central leader. Laterals should be well spaced, and should come from the main trunk in a wide V-angle for added strength: with age, wood becomes brittle and trees can shed large limbs. It is also a good idea, therefore, to reduce the spread of mature limbs periodically by shortening the longer branches.

Sweet chestnut trees are sometimes grown for their decorative furrowed bark as well as for their strange, conker-like fruits

Macadamia Nuts
Macadamia spp.

The Macadamia nut is usually regarded as *Macadamia integrifolia*. A native of Australia, it is now grown commercially throughout sub-tropical parts of the world. *M. integrifolia* bears creamy white flowers that are attractive to bees, and a smooth-skinned fruit containing a sweet and crisp white kernel tasting rather like a hazel nut.

In cooler climates macadamias may be grown as foliage plants under glass, and will survive as long as the winter temperature does not drop below 15°C (60°F). Plants may be put outside for the summer. However, they will need the space of the open garden if they are to develop fruit. Commercially

A macadamia nut tree will fruit successfully outdoors as long as the temperature stays above 15°C (60°F)

farmed trees will crop well for up to 50 years, starting around years five or six. If the tree is simply grown for decoration, and a few nuts annually, it can crop for 100 years or more.

Pruning requirements Grow as a single-stemmed tree with a clear trunk of 1m (3ft), with well space laterals. Regularly tip back the laterals to keep the tree in shape and to size; this will also encourage flowering shoots to develop. Mature trees tolerate hard pruning in spring.

Pistachio
Pistacia vera

Also known as the green almond, this nut has long been cultivated in Mediterranean and western Asian countries, and in more recent times it has become a successful commercial crop in the warmer states of the USA. To set fruit, male and female plants must be grown together at a ratio of 1:5.

In cool, temperate climates it must be grown under cover of glass.

Pruning requirements Train the main stem to form a trunk 1m (3ft) high before the branch system is formed. Prune in mid-summer. Laterals can become untidy, so should be thinned out regularly, but keep further pruning to a minimum as cuts neither heal quickly nor generate significant new growth.

Almond

Prunus dulcis

The common almond is usually grown for its early pink blossom, but in some years sets an excellent crop of nuts.

Pruning requirements The almond is best left unpruned, as it produces flower quite readily, and trees that are cut back hard are likely to be attacked by silver leaf disease and die back fungus, or they will start suckering – a most annoying habit, particularly if the tree is situated in a lawn. Young trees usually have their heads formed in the nursery, but may need a slight thinning of the shoots. Cut any crossing or crowded shoots clean out, and tip the leaders if not enough side breaks have formed.

Hazel (Cobnuts) & Filberts

Corylus avellana, C. maxima

Cobnuts and filberts are very closely related botanically, but for practical purposes are distinguished by the length of husk that encloses the nut. In the filbert this husk is as long, or longer, than the nut, which is hidden, but in the cobnut the husk is shorter and the nut is more or less exposed.

These nuts will thrive on practically all soil types, from stiff clay to light sand, acid

Almond trees flower and fruit early in the year, but if the weather is cold a crop of nuts is not guaranteed

Harvesting almonds

The nuts can be swept off the tree with a besom broom, and the husks will readily come away. The nuts themselves are very hard to split. Some gardeners resort to cracking them in an ordinary carpenter's vice; this is much safer than hammering, as they could fly off in all directions. The kernels should be dried off on newspaper for a few days and then stored in an airtight container.

If the whole nuts are stored, the shells must be dry and clean; otherwise fungi grow on them and may reach and damage the kernel. A hard nailbrush is a good way to clean the whole nuts, which should then be bleached in the sun for several days.

or alkaline. On rich soils they may tend to need more pruning, but they should certainly crop well. Two good varieties for garden planting are 'Kentish Cob', and 'Cosford' (the latter being a true hazel nut).

Pruning requirements They tend to make a lot of new wood growth within the framework of the tree and unless some of this is pruned, overcrowding of the branches develops. For good cropping results, and the largest nuts, it is best to treat the plants as single-stemmed trees with no main branches, only short, but effective, laterals.

Walnuts

Juglans regia

Trees that crop are usually inherited: seldom is it possible to plant and crop a tree within a lifetime! Varieties can be planted but it would be a wait of at least 20 years before the first few nuts are likely to appear. Avoid growing them at all if your garden is susceptible to late spring frosts.

Pruning requirements Commercial walnuts are usually grown as bushes, with open centres; this makes harvesting easier. In a garden setting, however, it is best to train trees to a central leader with laterals. Prune when in leaf, since the tree 'bleeds' less then.

Pruning Soft Fruits & Vines

The easiest types of fruit to grow and care for are the so-called soft fruits. Depending on the type and cultivar, and whether or not you can employ a greenhouse to give you earlier than normal crops, there is no reason why a small fruit garden should not provide a family with home-grown soft fruit for nine months of the year. And, unlike tree fruits, there will be room in every garden for at least one type of soft fruit.

Flavour is something hybridists have striven for over the years, along with cropping potential, weather tolerance and pest and disease resistance. But to most gardeners, the importance of taste outweighs many of the other considerations. Freshness, too, is a valuable asset, and if you are unable to grow your own plants, freshness can only be bought from a pick-your-own farm. Currants, gooseberries and many of the hybrid berries are frequently unavailable fresh from supermarkets, so to grow your own is the only way you can enjoy them without resorting to frozen, tinned or dried versions.

General cultivation

Soft fruits do come in a variety of sizes, shapes and styles: from the cane fruits (raspberries, blackberries and the many hybrid berries), and the bush fruits (black, red and white currants, gooseberries and blueberries), to vine fruits (grapes, kiwi and passion fruits) and to the low-growing herbaceous – that is, non-woody – strawberries. With such a wide variety of growing habits, there are also different cultural requirements: it pays to understand the fruits' needs; failure here will mean you could forfeit an entire year's fruiting potential.

The golden rules that apply to all soft fruits are:

• Enrich the soil at planting time with well-rotted manure or compost.
• Make sure you feed the plants each year, to a strict fertilizer regime that will vary according to the soil condition and the fruits you are growing.

Both of these instructions point to one thing: soft fruits are hungry plants. This is not surprising when you think of what they do to earn their keep: they produce bunches and bunches of richly tasting fruits to keep us happy, and this uses up all their energy and resources; it is only fair that we should feed them!

Cane Fruits

The name fairly adequately describes the growth habit of these fruits. Each type throws up sturdy canes, often densely thorned to protect them in the wild from marauding animals, but which can pose a painful problem for gardeners if not noticed!

The most widely grown cane fruit is the raspberry, followed in popularity by the blackberry, the loganberry and then a variety of modern hybrid berries, including the boysenberry, tayberry and veitchberry. The one thing these plants all have in common is that they start to fruit in the second year after planting.

Raspberries are a good example of a popular cane fruit. They look good and are very tasty

Blackberries & Loganberries

Blackberries have been grown in gardens for centuries, but closely related, and much newer, is the loganberry. Its fruits are rather larger than the blackberry, the plants are somewhat smaller, and the crops are generally heavier.

Pruning requirements

The thornless varieties of both fruits are much appreciated at harvest time and when it comes to pruning!

1 – Set out new plants in late autumn, and straight away cut them down to 23cm (0in).
2 – During the following summer tie in new canes, as they appear, on to the supporting wires and into a fan shape. These canes will not fruit until the following year.
3 – During the second spring after planting prune back the weak tips to leave the canes at a comfortable height for picking, usually about 1.5m (5ft).
4 – Four months later fruit can be harvested, after which tie the new, young canes into the open, centre framework of the plant, and

along the top wire. By doing this you will be keeping the old canes quite separate from the new.
5 – When harvesting is finished in autumn, cut out all of the fruited canes to near ground level and release the new rods into the fan shape. Make sure they are tied in securely. The renewal process is now under way.

Blackberries grow easily in the wild but have also been cultivated in gardens for centuries

Hybrid Berries

Prune all of the following as for blackberries.

Boysenberry The black-red fruits are similar to a long-stalked loganberry, but are somewhat rounder. Canes can reach a height of 2.4m (8ft). Some growers believe that the boysenberry is a cross between raspberries and blackberries, whilst others think that the loganberry is in the ancestry. The fruit

Loganberries are a relatively new innovation in the world of cane fruit and are becoming more and more popular

Wineberries

Often known as the Japanese wineberry, this fruit is not a modern hybrid, but a distinct species: *Rubus phoenicolasius*, and was first discovered growing wild in the Japanese mountains. It is a striking plant, often grown for its ornamental appeal alone. The canes, which can grow to 2m (6ft) in a good soil, are thickly covered in bright red spines that make the plant stand out well in an otherwise bare winter garden. The bright red fruits resemble smallish blackberries in shape. Prune as for blackberries.

withstands drought well, so is an excellent choice for a sunny, dry spot in the garden.

Tayberry A cross between an American bramble and a raspberry, perhaps best described as a super loganberry; it is much heavier cropping, by up to half as much again. The fruits are much the same colour, but rather less acid to taste. Set plants 2.4m (8ft) apart.

Veitchberry A cross between a large fruited blackberry and a raspberry, great for

Tayberries are similar to loganberries but sport even larger, heavier fruits in greater numbers

filling the soft-fruit gap in summer, between the end of summer-fruiting raspberries and the beginning of the blackberry season. Berries are carried on vigorous canes, and have a fine, mild flavour.

Raspberries

Raspberries are not difficult to grow, and apart from eating the fruits fresh off the canes, they are also suitable for both jam making and freezing. One of the reasons for their wide popularity is that they will grow almost anywhere, provided they are planted on well-drained soil. If looked after, the plants may be expected to provide worthwhile crops for 10–12 years before needing to be replaced.

There are two basic kinds of raspberries: the more common summer-fruiting types, and the less common autumn-fruiting types.

Summer fruiting

There are dozens of varieties available to the amateur gardener, and some of the best for flavour and cropping potential are 'Glen Prosen' (spine-free canes, heavy cropper); 'Redsetter' (large fruits, good flavour); and 'Malling Admiral' (arguably the best for flavour). There is, also, a yellow-fruiting form: 'Summergold' (a novel raspberry with attractive fruits).

1 – Cut back the shoots, or canes, to about 30cm (12in) at planting time, usually during late autumn. New canes will grow from the base of the plants during the following summer.
2 – Throughout summer you should remove any weak canes and tie in the others to support wires so that they are about 10cm (4in) apart. There need only be two support wires, at 60cm (2ft) and 1.5m (5ft) from the ground. They should be pulled taut between sturdy posts at each end.
3 – Once the plants are established, simply cut the fruited canes to ground level as soon as cropping ceases, and tie in the strongest replacement canes. It is best not to retain

Tip raspberry canes in the spring

more than five or six from each plant, selecting the strongest-looking, and ideally so that there is some 8–10cm (3–4in) between them.

4 – In spring, when these retained canes have reached just past the topmost wire on the support system they should be tipped: you can safely leave some 15cm (6in) or so above the wire.

Autumn fruiting

These are varieties of raspberry that bear fruit in mid-summer in the normal way, but in addition produce flowers on current season's new canes, the fruit of which ripen from late summer onwards. There are far fewer varieties, and two worth mentioning are: 'Autumn Bliss' (exceptionally heavy cropper, with sturdy canes that in a sheltered garden may not even need supporting); and 'Ruby' (high quality fruits with good taste). Autumn fruiting raspberries do not crop as heavily as summer ones, but they do so at a quieter time of the year.

1 – Follow steps 1 and 2 for summer fruiting raspberries, as the initial pruning is the same.

2 – Subsequent attention is different because fruit is set on wood produced the same year. In late winter, just before new growth starts to break, cut all canes back to ground level. Fruit will then be carried the following autumn at the tips of the new canes produced since pruning.

A word about strawberries

The most popular type of soft fruit, the strawberry, does not really fall within the remit of this book, as it is not a 'woody' plant, and so does not require pruning in the conventional sense. Having said that, there is a degree of cutting back required:

Flowers If, for any reason, a strawberry plant is poor, the flower trusses should be cut off with scissors so that the plants may devote their energies to building up crowns to produce the following year's fruits.

Runners From late spring onwards runners will start appearing, and these will root readily in the soil. You will need to decide whether to maintain individual plants, or to create a matted bed of plants. Single plants are easier to keep free from weeds, and the fruits may be larger, but there are likely to be fewer of them.

Leaves On healthy, vigorous plants use a pair of shears to cut off the old leaves, but take care not to cut into the crown of the plant. Do this in mid-autumn.

Bush Fruits

Unlike cane fruits, the bush forms produce a framework of branches or stems. They may come from a single stem or trunk (as in the case of redcurrants and gooseberries), or they may be multi-stemmed (as with blackcurrants).

Blackcurrants

The blackcurrant really should be in every garden! The high vitamin C content of the fruits, together with the fact that plants are tolerant of poor soil conditions, the crops come early and yields are high for the space the plant occupies, all give the blackcurrant special value. The life-span of a bush that is well cared for is about 15 years, and youthful, vigorous bushes give the best crops.

'Ben Lomond' is probably the most widely grown variety for the amateur, and is also popular in commerce. It is moderately vigorous, and so requires the minimum of pruning. It is late flowering, and the flavour of its currants is very good. 'Ben Sarek' forms a small, compact bush, producing a high-yielding crop of good-flavoured currants. The branches are rather spreading, however, and it may be necessary to support them with plant stakes, or a series of bamboo canes with strings between them.

Pruning requirements

In general, blackcurrants produce the best fruits on the previous year's wood, but they will also crop on older wood:

1 – Cut down new plants drastically, to about 2.5cm (1in) from ground level, at planting time. This will cause vigorous new shoots to develop the following spring and summer but any fruit that forms should not be picked during this time. From this initial cutting back no pruning will be required until after the plant has fruited.

2 – Between late autumn and mid-winter – two years from planting – cut out about one-third of the fruited branches back to almost ground level. Also remove damaged and weak growths.

3 – After the next summer, and in subsequent years, each annual pruning involves the removal of about three complete branches of old wood, followed by the removal of other fruited branches back to vigorous new laterals.

Blackcurrants are amazing fruits that will grow just about anywhere and will last for years

Red and white currants

These two fruits vary only in the colour of the fruits; in every detail of cultivation they should be treated similarly. Beside the normal redcurrant jelly, a raspberry and redcurrant jam is well worth trying.

The best varieties of redcurrant for the amateur are 'Jonkheer van Tets' (an early ripening Dutch variety bearing heavy crops in long trusses), and 'Laxton's No. 1' (earlier to flower and crop, with bright red berries on long trusses; it has the added advantage of being somewhat resistant to mildew disease). There is only really one white currant of note and this is 'White Versailles', a heavy cropper with large, pale yellow fruits; it makes a strong, vigorous upright bush.

Pruning requirements

Both currants carry crops on short spurs from a permanent framework of old wood, and so are pruned differently from blackcurrants – more in line with gooseberries.

1 – It is best to plant in early autumn, not spring. Rub off any suckers or buds on the roots and stem, as these will be a constant problem afterwards if left to grow. Leave a good, clean stem of about 15cm (6in).
2 – The initial pruning is similar to gooseberries: cut the branches back by about half, to outward-pointing buds, and cut out any weak growths.
3 – From the second year onwards cut back all of the leaders by around half. At the same time, cut back all side shoots to 2.5cm (1in), or less. This is done to encourage the fruits, which are carried on spurs at the base of the side shoots.
4 – Summer pruning is beneficial in helping to ripen the young wood, as well as the fruit itself. Soon after mid-summer shorten the laterals to about five leaves.

Whitecurrants require the same growing conditions and pruning treatment as redcurrants

Cordon-trained currants

Red and white currants may be trained as single-stemmed, vertical 'cordons'. Here you will need to plant the currants next to a wall, or post-and-wire support with the wires spaced at 30cm (12in) intervals.

At planting time cut back the leading shoot by half, and all other shoots to one bud.

In early summer prune the young side shoots to five leaves, and tie in the leading shoot.

During the following winter prune back the side shoots to one or two buds. Also, shorten the leading shoot by one third of new growth (this done each winter until the plant has reached the desired height).

When mature, the leader should be stopped at five leaves in early summer, and the side shoots pruned back to one or two buds of the old growth in the winter.

Gooseberries

The gooseberry is the first fruit to ripen in the new growing year. The fruit should be thinned in late spring, and the thinning used for cooking. The remainder should be left to swell near to full size and then used for pies, freezing and jamming. But to appreciate a gooseberry in all its glory, some should be left to ripen fully. They become sweet and richly flavoured.

There are several excellent garden varieties. 'Invicta' is immune to a fungal disease known as American gooseberry mildew, which can wreak havoc in a gooseberry patch. It is a heavy cropper, with large, oval, pale green berries of good flavour. 'Leveller' is possibly the best-tasting gooseberry, but is a weak grower and needs careful cultivation; 'Whinham's Industry' has reddish fruits, almost purple when ripe; well-flavoured but susceptible to mildew.

Gooseberries are mainly used for cooking, but are also delicious raw when allowed to ripen fully

Pruning requirements

Gooseberries fruit on two-year-old shoots and on any spurs that form on the growths that remain after the thinning out of undesirable wood. Formative training should be to establish a well-spaced bush on a single stem rising 15–20cm (6–8in) from ground level.

1 – Just after planting, between late autumn and mid-winter, cut all branches back by about half.

TIP

Worcesterberries
This hybrid fruit resembles a large, rather drooping gooseberry bush; the arching branches carry small, near-black, gooseberry-shaped berries. The origin of the plant is a mystery; some say it is a cross between a blackcurrant and a gooseberry, while others call it the American currant (*Ribes divaricatum*).

2 – One year later select eight healthy branches and cut these back by half.
3 – A year later prune the leaders by half, but this time leave the laterals unpruned.
4 – From now on the only major pruning required is the complete removal of weak shoots and the occasional old branch. Try always to keep the centre of the bush open, and the branches away from the ground. And each summer shorten all laterals to about five leaves, to encourage the formation of fruit buds.

Gooseberries can also be grown as single-stemmed cordons; train and prune as described for red currants.

Some varieties of gooseberry sport attractive red fruits instead of the more usual green

TIP

The profitable life of a gooseberry is 12-15 years, although some bushes crop for much longer than this. When old bushes make little growth it pays to replace them with new, young plants, but preferably in another part of the garden. Rather like ornamental rose bushes, gooseberries do not perform well when planted on soil that has previously grown the same type of plant.

Blueberries

More correctly referred to as the American highbush blueberry, this is a highly nutritious fruit, with many health-giving properties (see box). The berries are up to 2cm (¾in) across, and blue-black when fully ripe. The outside of the berries are covered in a waxy white 'bloom' which gives them the appearance of being pale blue.

Their taste can be considered bland when eaten raw, but the flavour strengthens during cooking; they are good for bottling and freezing. 'Bluecrop' is an early cultivar, with high quality firm, light blue fruits. 'Berkeley' is a mid-season form, with spreading, highly productive branches.

These are slower growers compared to other soft fruits, but having said this, plants may reach 2m (6ft) or more in an ideal soil. This is the crucial point: they need a very acid soil (they are in the same plant family as heathers and rhododendrons). They also like plenty of moisture around the roots in summer. They are decorative too, with some varieties offering red and gold autumn leaf tints.

Pruning requirements

Blueberries are grown as multi-stemmed bushes, rather like blackcurrants, and the berries are carried on side shoots of wood formed the previous year.

No regular pruning is necessary until cropping begins, which probably will not be before the third year. However, failure to do any pruning after this time will result in irregular, individual berries rather than heavy clusters.

From the third year onwards make it an annual winter job to cut back two or three of the oldest fruited branches, to either a vigorous young shoot, or completely to ground level. Remove dead or damaged branches close to the base.

'Berkeley' is a cultivar that is sometimes reluctant to produce sturdy new growth following a hard pruning, but fortunately it crops reasonably well on older wood.

Blueberries are renowned for their many health-giving properties

The blueberry 'superfood'

One serving of blueberries, that equates to a large handful, provides as many antioxidants – chemical compounds which help ward off illnesses – as the equivalent of five servings of either carrots, apples, broccoli or squash. Blueberries are rich in vitamin C and E, both of which are known to 'feed the brain'. There are hopes that blueberries will also help sufferers fight dementia and Alzheimer's disease. One ingredient found in the fruits, pterostilbene, is believed to be helpful in lowering cholesterol levels; it has already been shown to help fight cancer and diabetes.

Vines

Vines are climbing plants, which use tendrils to haul themselves up and over structures. This is the closest the plant world gets to something resembling muscular action in animals, and the grapevine is probably the best example. Its tendrils are like long leaf stalks without leaves, which can weave about like the 'legs' of an octopus until they touch something that feels promising as a handhold. The cells on one side of the tip then multiply with speed, whilst those on the other side stay as they were, making the tip curve, usually around its target. The three main fruiting vines are grapes, of course, followed by kiwi fruits and then passion fruits.

Grapes

Vitis vinifera

There are many different types of grape. To start with there are, of course, black (more purple-brown in reality) or white (actually green) grapes, but beyond this they can be further divided. There are sweet or dessert grapes, there are wine (acid) grapes, and then there are a few varieties that are dual-purpose. Within these divisions there are varieties that ripen early, mid- or late season: so it pays to know what you want before you plant!

Indoor grapevines

Anyone with an average-sized greenhouse can grow excellent grapes. Indoor grapes like their roots to be cool; this is why traditionally vines are planted with their roots outside of the greenhouse, with their stems carried through a hole in the structure to produce leaf and fruit inside. Train the vine up wires strung between upright posts high up, or near the roof, to ensure they receive as much air and sunshine as possible.

Look for the white varieties 'Foster's Seedling' and 'Muscat of Alexandria'. The latter variety is arguably the sweetest dessert grape of all, but it does like warm conditions. Of the black varieties, look for 'Napoleon' and the old favourite 'Black Hamburg'.

Pruning requirements

It is best to buy a 'fruiting vine', so that one does not have to wait years for a crop.

1 – Keep the vine in its pot over the first winter, and about a month before planting it in the spring, prune it so that about 30cm (1ft) of stem remains.
2 – Settle the vine into its planted position. From this stem allow a single, strong shoot

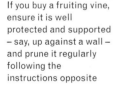

If you buy a fruiting vine, ensure it is well protected and supported – say, up against a wall – and prune it regularly following the instructions opposite

to grow up, pinching out any laterals at two leaves.

3 – Stop the leader when it is about 1.8m (6ft) tall. Then choose a strong shoot as a result of the stopping, and train it along the roof of the greenhouse as the leader.

4 – The following winter, prune back the leading stem to about 1.5m (5ft), and the side shoots to two buds.

5 – A year later, stop the leader when it reaches the apex of the greenhouse, and stop the side shoots when they are about 60cm (2ft) long.

6 – In spring, thin out the laterals so that there is one every 30–38cm (12–15in) along the rod. Each lateral should now produce a bunch of grapes, and be stopped two leaves beyond the bunch.

7 – The following winter the laterals are again cut back to two buds.

You are now into the six-monthly summer and winter pruning cycle. In winter, when the plant is dormant, you should aim to remove old, dead, diseased and damaged wood, and to encourage the vine to produce masses of new spring and summer growth. Then, in the summer, the new growth is tipped to prevent crowding and to keep the vine within bounds.

Outdoor grapevines

In a hot summer, good crops can be had from outdoor vines. White varieties such as 'Muller Thurgau' and 'Siegerrebe' are popular, as are the black 'Concord' and 'Brant'. The latter is very vigorous, hardy and bears heavy crops of smallish berries.

A position sheltered from cold winds is needed for outdoor grapes, and preferably facing south or west. Grow them against a wall or on supporting wires, and pruning is similar to that of indoor kinds, except that subsidiary rods can be left to develop off the main rod.

An espalier vine can be grown, with rods each side of the main stem at intervals of about 38cm (15in). Allow laterals to grow only on the upper sides of the rods, spaced at about 45cm (18in).

If your vine fruits too abundantly, thin the grapes with scissors to reduce the burden on the growing plant (see also page 101)

Thinning grapes

There are two types of thinning.

Reducing bunches The first is something that every grower should adhere to: as fruit develops it is necessary to thin bunches to one per stem to allow the fruit to reach their maximum size and to aid air circulation. Healthy rods should carry one bunch per spur, that is a bunch per 23–30cm (9–12in) of rod. Weak rods should only be allowed to carry a bunch every other spur, all other flower trusses having been pinched off.

Thinning within bunches The second type of thinning applies to the individual grapes within a bunch. Sometimes if the bunches are left to their own devices they will become crowded with masses of small berries. This is when you should thin the bunch, using a pair of grape scissors specially developed for the job (and available only through specialist dealers), however any sharp-pointed scissors will do. It is best to thin out the berries when they are just a 3–4mm (⅛in) across, and then again if necessary when they are the size of small peas. Eventually the berries should be about 2.5cm (1in) apart: this will give you an evenly-spaced bunch with well-shaped 'shoulders'. After each thinning process you will think that the bunch looks sparse, but it is surprising how it thickens up as the berries swell.

Kiwi Fruit

Actinidia deliciosa

Although this used to be known as the Chinese gooseberry, as it is actually New Zealand from where most of the world's stock come, fruit marketeers have successfully changed the plant's common name. In little more than two decades the pretty, green-fleshed, black-seeded fruits have come from nowhere, to the top of the fruit league.

To produce fruits well outdoors the kiwi needs to be grown in a sunny, sheltered position. The plant produces attractive trailing vines, sometimes 9m (28ft) long, and although growing under glass would be more appropriate, there are not many of us with greenhouses large enough – serious growers with the space could choose instead to use a long polytunnel.

Male and female vines are necessary for the flowers to be pollinated, and thus produce fruit, but as the plants take a while to become established, do not expect any fruit until four or five years after planting.

Pruning requirements

Growing in espalier form is a good idea, with wires spaced at 45cm (18in) apart; vines trained in this way have to be spur pruned.

Careful pruning is necessary if you are to prevent the vine from producing too much stem and leaf growth at the expense of flowers and fruit.

1 – The fruits are carried on wood made the previous year, so fruited side shoots should be cut back to three or four buds; do this when the vine is dormant in late winter.
2 – To keep the vine within bounds, cut back excessive growth to just above any fruit, while it is growing in the summer.

Passion Fruit

Passiflora spp.

These plants are usually grown for their highly ornate flowers – and there are many dozens of cultivars and species. Some of them, however, have excellent fruiting capabilities as well. Most forms are tropical or sub-tropical, so keep them well sheltered.

The most common hardy passionflower plant is *Passiflora caerulea*; its plum-sized orange fruits are, however, insipid, slightly blackberry-flavoured. Better fruits are to be had on *P. actinia* (will tolerate slight frost; slightly acid, grape-flavoured fruits); *P. incarnata* (very hardy; slightly acid fruits); *P. membranacea* (slightly frost tolerant; sweet fruits), and *P. edulis* (needs greenhouse conditions, the best choice for fruiting).

Pruning requirements

Vines are capable of reaching great lengths and height, so should be supported on a series of sturdy wires or trellis: when laden with fruit the stems can be exceptionally heavy. Pruning is not difficult.

1 – In early spring, pinch out the tips of the side shoots.
2 – In winter cut back shoots that have borne fruit that year.
3 – Any other pruning will be to keep the vine from becoming too crowded and overgrown. Carry out maintenance pruning of this nature in mid-spring.

Kiwi plants will only bear fruit if both male and female vines are planted – and then only quite slowly

The Pruner's Glossary

Pruning, as with most specialist subjects, has a vocabulary of its own. Certain terms, such as root and bud, are familiar to even non-gardeners. Yet there are plenty of words that, without some explanation, are likely to leave the novice gardener perplexed. Here, some of the terms used throughout this book are explained to help reduce the confusion.

Adventitious bud A bud that arises on a stem or branch, but in an abnormal position, usually in response to a wound.

Alternate The way in which shoots, buds and/or leaves are arranged alternately on either side of a stem (see also Opposite).

Axil The angle between the upper side of a leaf and the stem from which it emerges; the normal position for lateral or axillary buds.

Bark-ringing Removing a narrow strip, or 'ring', of bark from the trunk of an over-vigorous or unfruitful tree, to check root growth and induce flower and fruit production. The strip of bark should extend about three quarters of the way around the tree; do not complete the 'ring' as this would kill the tree, preventing the upward flow of nutrients from the root area.

Biennial bearing Fruit trees that bear heavily one year, but scarcely at all the next.

Blind shoot A shoot that does not develop properly, in which the terminal bud dies and no further growth takes place.

Break Growth made from a once dormant bud.

Budding Where a bud of one variety is inserted into the growing stem of another variety. The new bud will eventually grow and form branches, but of a variety or cultivar different to that of the rootstock.

Callus Superficial corky tissue produced by a plant to heal a wound.

Coppice Some trees, such as hazel (Corylus) and sweet chestnut (Castanea), are grown for their young stems, or brushwood, which can be used for 'chestnut fencing', 'wattle hurdles', stakes and other rustic uses. As the crop is collected they are cut down to within 30cm (1ft) or so of the ground, a process that is repeated at intervals of five to seven years. Such a planting is referred to as a coppice, and the act of pruning in this way is known as coppicing.

Cordon A plant trained as a single main stem by regular spur pruning. U-shaped or double cordons have two such main stems. Most often referred to in the cultivation of fruits, such as apples, pears and some bush fruits like gooseberries.

Crown The main branch system of a tree.

Cultivar The term used to distinguish a cultivated plant form from a botanical variety. The cultivar is usually bred for its superior qualities as a decorative plant, whereas the botanical variety may be a naturally growing form with lesser qualities (although this is not exclusively the case). Cultivars are distinguished by using capitals for the initial letters of their distinctive names, and by putting these names in single inverted commas e.g. *Philadelphus coronarius* 'Aureus'.

Deadhead The removal, by hand or with the use of a tool, of dead flowers and unripe seed, to prevent waste of the plant's energy resources.

Disbudding The removal of surplus flower buds to produce a better bloom from the main bud.

Dormant bud A bud that remains inactive until stimulated through pruning or accidental damage. Such a bud is generally formed in a leaf axil, although the leaf may have been shed some time in the past.

Deadheading improves a plant's health

Opposite buds

Espalier A plant, similar to a cordon in its pruning and fruit production, but trained with a vertical stem and horizontal tiers of branches. This is a common form of training for apples, pears and other forms of top fruit.

Eye A dormant growth bud, particularly on vines and roses.

Fan Fruiting or ornamental tree or shrub, trained against a wall or support, where all the branches radiate from a short central trunk.

Feathers Lateral growths, really no more than short twigs, coming from the main stem of a tree.

Fireblight A disease that attacks many woody members of the rose family (Rosaceae). In late spring and early summer dead shoots with dead, blackened leaves can be seen, giving the appearance that branches have been burnt.

Framework Formation of branches in the crown of a tree.

Grafting The joining together of two totally separate plants to form a single new individual, having the root system (or rootstock) of one plant and the shoot or single bud of another (the scion).

Growth bud A bud that gives rise to a shoot, as distinct from a fruit bud that produces a flower.

Half-standard Tree with a clear stem of 1–1.2m (3–4ft). The branch framework develops on top of this. A half-standard rose usually has 90cm (3ft) of bare stem.

Hard pruning The removal of a large amount of wood from a tree or shrub.

Internode A node is the point on a stem where a leaf or leaves arise; so the internode is the section of stem between two nodes.

Lateral A side shoot or branch (as distinct from a leader), which grows from lateral buds on a main or leading stem.

Leader Generally the top-most growth on the framework of a tree or shrub. It should be the dominant growth and thus stronger than the other laterals. One or more leading shoots may also be found on the laterals.

Leg A short, clear length of main stem on a shrub before branching is allowed to take place.

Lorette This is a method of pruning apples and pears, in which the leaders are tipped in spring and the laterals are cut back almost to the base according to their thickness and age, at various times in summer.

Maiden A one-year-old tree or shrub or, occasionally with fruit trees, a term used to describe one-year-old growth.

Opposite This, literally, is the opposite to alternate. Shoots, buds and/or leaves are arranged so that they are opposite to each other on the stem (see also Alternate).

Ornamentals These are plants that are grown for their appearance rather than for food or commercial reasons.

Pinch back Also known as 'stopping', this is the removal of young shoots early in the growing season, usually done by hand.

Pleaching Technique of forming a dense hedge by interweaving the branches of well-spaced plants, usually such trees as lime (Tilia) or hornbeam (Carpinus), and often leaving bare trunks as 'stilts'. A pleached alley is a garden walk lined with pleached trees.

Pollard The name given to any tree that has been repeatedly pruned very severely, in other words which has been lopped. Pollarding is the term used to describe the lopping of such a tree.

Recurrent flowering The repeated production of flowers, more or less in succession, during one season.

Renewal pruning Pruning to obtain a constant supply of young shoots, usually on apple and pear trees, so that freedom of flowering and vigour are maintained.

Reversion A condition on a variegated plant where a green shoot grows away at the expense of the variegated shoots.

Ripe wood A branch or shoot that is lignified (turned to wood from a green, sappy growth). See Unripe (or semi-ripe) wood.

Rod The name for the main, woody stem of a grapevine.

Root pruning The removal of a part of a root system of any plant to induce better growth or the better production of fruit/flower buds.

Rootstock The root system on to which a scion is budded or grafted.

Rubbing out The removal of buds and young shoots by rubbing the hand along the branch or trunk.

Scion A bud or shoot of a desired variety that is grafted to a rootstock. It is from the scion that a framework of branches will arise.

Silver leaf A disease attacking a wide range of trees and shrubs, but particularly members of the rose family (Rosaceae), where the leaves take on a leaden or silvery appearance.

Snag A short stump of a branch left after incorrect pruning.

Sport A plant propagated from a tree or shrub branch that developed differently from the parent plant in size, shape, colour, etc.

Spur This is a short branch system that usually carries clusters of flower buds. Natural spurs are short laterals with the nodes close together; an induced or artificial spur is created after a specific pruning technique.

Standard Tree with a clear stem of 1.8–2.4m

(6–8ft). Like the half-standard, a branch system will develop above the clear stem. A standard rose, however, usually has only 1.2m (4ft) of clear stem.

Sucker Although this term has several horticultural meanings, it is generally used to describe a shoot growing from a root or stem below ground. Also applies to a stem arising from the rootstock of a grafted plant.

Tap root A plant's main root.

Terminal bud Growth bud at the end of an unpruned shoot.

Thinning The reduction of the number of branches in an overcrowded system, to facilitate a good circulation of air and allow sunlight and warmth to ripen foliage and fruits.

Tip-bearer An apple tree that produces fruit buds on the tips of shoots instead of on spurs or laterals.

Topiary The art of training and trimming trees and shrubs to clearly defined three-dimensional shapes. These are often seen as birds, animals and even pieces of furniture. Geometric shapes such as cones, archways, globes and spirals are also common.

Truss A cluster of flowers or fruit.

Union The junction between rootstock and scion, or between two scions grafted together.

Unripe (or semi-ripe) wood Shoots in which the process of lignification is not complete by autumn (see Ripe wood).

Water shoots Vigorous, sappy growths, which develop from adventitious buds on the trunk, or within the older framework of the tree.

Windrock This is the loosening of a plant's root system by strong winds. It can be avoided by planting firmly, staking securely, or cutting back some of the plant's longer growths (where appropriate).

Trim topiary regularly with hand shears

The Pruner's Year

Creating the following lists of plants, and the appropriate times to prune them, has not been easy. It is impossible to lay down hard and fast rules on such timings – the weather, soil and local environments are all so variable. Additionally, there are frequently plant species within the same genus that require pruning at a completely different period of the year. Therefore, there can be no set programme of 'what to do and when'. However, these few pages should act as a general guide to the approximate pruning times for the majority of the most commonly found garden trees, shrubs and fruits.

One important thing to note: if it is recommended that a plant should be pruned in a certain season, and this is also the usual flowering season (e.g. Rhododendron, under 'Spring'), you should always undertake the pruning after flowering is finished. If you prune before the flowering takes place, you are likely to forfeit the vast majority, or even the year's entire flowering potential.

Finally, if a specific plant is not included on these pages, it is reasonably safe to assume that the timing of any pruning is not critical, but do check with the more detailed pruning instructions provided in the plant directory section of this book.

Winter is the best time to prune *Parrotia persica*

Winter

THE ORNAMENTAL GARDEN:
Prune the following:
Acer, horse chestnut (Aesculus), snowy mespilus (Amelanchier), Ampelopsis, birch (Betula), butterfly bush (*Buddleja davidii*), hornbeam (Carpinus), *Clematis orientalis*, *C. tangutica*, *C. jackmanii*, *C. viticella*, smokebush (Cotinus), thorns (Crataegus), winter-flowering heathers (Erica) after they have flowered, hardy fuchsias, *Hebe* 'Autumn Glory', sea buckthorn (Hippophaë), Hypericum, Laburnum, Parrotia, pine (Pinus), poplar (Populus), elder (Sambucus), *Spiraea japonica*, summer-flowering Viburnum, Vitis, Wisteria.

Cornus alba and *Salix alba* should be pruned in alternate years at the end of winter when the leaves start to emerge.

Late winter is the conventional time to prune bush roses, but they could instead be pruned in late autumn.

Other tasks:
• Brush snow off trees and shrubs to avoid stems and branches snapping.
• Clip ivy (Hedera) to keep it under control.
• Check tree stakes and ties to make sure that they are not so tight as to restrict the plant's growth.

THE FRUIT GARDEN:
Prune the following:
Apples, pears, gooseberries, red and white currants, newly planted blackcurrants, autumn fruiting raspberries, blueberries, quinces, outdoor peaches and nectarines, medlars, fruiting vines.

Other tasks:
• Spur back laterals on hazel nuts as soon as the catkins have withered.
• Cut back newly planted raspberries to 15cm (6in) or so from the ground.
• Tip back unripened shoots of raspberries and blackberries.

Spring

THE ORNAMENTAL GARDEN:

Prune the following:

Abelia, *Abutilon* x *suntense*, tree of heaven (Ailanthus), strawberry tree (Arbutus), spotted laurel (Aucuba), Berberis (evergreen), box (Buxus), Callicarpa, ling (Calluna), Camellia, Campsis, blue spiraea (*Caryopteris* x *clandonensis*), Indian bean tree (Catalpa), Ceanothus (deciduous), hardy plumbago (*Ceratostigma willmottianum*), *Clematis montana*, *C. chrysocoma* and *C. macropetala*, Clerodendrum, winter dogwoods (Cornus), hazel (Corylus), Cotoneaster, pineapple broom (*Cytisus battandieri*), St Dabeoc's heath (Daboecia), *Daphne mezereum*, Deutzia, Diervilla, oleaster (Elaeagnus), Escallonia, Euonymus, false castor oil plant (Fatsia), golden bells (Forsythia), tassel bush (Garrya), Gaultheria, broadwood (Griselinia), Hebe, tree hollyhock (*Hibiscus syriacus*), Hydrangea, holly (Ilex), jasmine (Jasminum), Jew's mallow (Kerria), bay (Laurus), lavender (Lavandula), tree mallow (Lavatera), Californian fuchsia (Leycesteria), privet (Ligustrum), evergreen climbing honeysuckle (Lonicera), Mahonia, myrtle (Myrtus), olive (Olea), Osmanthus, Pachysandra, passion flower (Passiflora), Pernettya, Perowskia, Phlomis, Photinia, Phygelius, Pittosporum, Potentilla, ornamental Prunus, firethorn (Pyracantha), oak (Quercus), sumach (Rhus), flowering currant (Ribes), Rhododendron, rosemary (Rosmarinus), ornamental bramble (Rubus), butcher's broom (Ruscus), rue (Ruta), willow (Salix), sage (*Salvia officinalis*), cotton lavender (Santolina) if grown just for foliage, Christmas box (Sarcococca), Schizophragma, Senecio (including Brachyglottis), Skimmia, Solanum, mountain ash (Sorbus), Spanish broom (Spartium), snowberry (Symphoricarpos), yew (Taxus), arborvitae (Thuja), thyme (Thymus), Trachelospermum, winter-flowering Viburnum, gorse (*Ulex europaeus*).

  Also prune bamboos and ornamental grasses.

Other tasks:
- Trim evergreen trees and shrubs to shape.
- Clip hedges where necessary, but check for nesting birds first.
- Deadhead daffodils, tulips and rhododendrons, and any early-flowering perennials (such as Helleborus and Bergenia).
- Remove rose suckers.
- Tie in new growths of climbing and rambler roses, and other climbers requiring it.

THE FRUIT GARDEN:

Prune the following:

Morello cherries, loquat, figs.

Other tasks:
- Remove raspberry suckers unless they are required for propagation.
- Thin badly placed branches on all stone fruits, but leave plums until summer.
- Thin fan-trained peaches.
- Thin fruits of gooseberries, peaches, nectarines and apricots, and apple varieties that mature early – the fruits should be 15cm (6in) or so apart.
- Remove any mildewed branches on apple and pear trees.
- Remove any leaves with peach leaf curl disease (affecting mainly peaches, nectarines and almonds, but can also appear on other top fruits).

Euonymus japonicus 'Chollipo' will benefit from a tidying up during spring

Summer

THE ORNAMENTAL GARDEN:
Prune the following:
Abutilon x *suntense* (if not done in late spring), Acacia, Berberis (deciduous), *Buddleja globosa*, Ceanothus (evergreen), Celastrus, winter sweet (Chimonanthus), rock or sun roses (Cistus), broom (Cytisus, but not *Cytisus battandieri*), tulip tree (Liriodendron), Magnolia, tree peony (Paeonia), Paulownia, mock orange (Philadelphus), rambler roses, Wisteria.

Other tasks:
• Deadhead roses, herbaceous perennials and butterfly bushes (Buddleja).
• Remove rose suckers.
• Trim hedges as required.
• Cut back over-vigorous climbers.

THE FRUIT GARDEN:
Prune the following:
Trained apples and pears; gooseberries and red and white currants; sweet cherry, apricot, peach, nectarine, plum, damson and walnut trees; summer raspberries (after cropping).

Other tasks:
• Thin shoots of Morello cherries.
• Thin fruits of apples, pears and plums now that the natural 'drop' has passed.
• Remove water shoots on apples and pears.
• Check grape supports are sufficient to hold the weight of the crop.
• Check plums for silver leaf disease; if this is suspected, cut out the affected branch, well back to healthy wood, and burn it.
• Remove large, unripened fruit from outdoor figs, to leave the small ones for next year's crop.
• Pick apples and pears as they mature.

During the summer, pick pears as they mature to avoid fallen fruit

Remove unwanted growth of climbers in autumn to reduce the weight on the supporting structure

Autumn

THE ORNAMENTAL GARDEN:
Prune the following:
Bottle brush (Callistemon), shrubby honeysuckle (Lonicera), shrub and species roses, cotton lavender (Santolina) if grown for its flowers.

Other tasks:
• Remove dead stems and foliage of herbaceous perennials.
• Cut back bush roses by half, to prevent windrock.
• Remove large tree branches where necessary.
• Tie in shoots of climbers.
• Remove unwanted growth from Virginia creeper (*Parthenocissus tricuspidata*), after leaf fall, and ivy (Hedera).
• Cut back side shoots of flowering quince (Chaenomeles).
• Remove any damaged or broken tree or shrub branches.
• Check tree ties and stakes are not too tight.
• Clean, repair and oil/grease where necessary pruning tools and equipment.

THE FRUIT GARDEN:
Prune the following:
Blackberries, hybrid berries, autumn-fruiting raspberries, black currants, gooseberries, wineberries, mulberry, apple and pear trees (all after leaf fall).

Other tasks:
• Harvest remaining apples and pears.
• Remove any mildewed branches on apple and pear trees.
• Tie-in replacement canes of raspberries and blackberries.
• Check tree ties and stakes are not too tight.

Index

Acknowledgements

Thanks to Coolings Nurseries for their continued cooperation and assistance with the photography in this book, including the loan of tools and much specialist equipment. Special thanks go to: Sandra Gratwick. Coolings Nurseries Ltd., Rushmore Hill, Knockholt, Kent, TN14 7NN. Tel: 00 44 1959 532269; email: coolings@coolings.co.uk; website: www.coolings.co.uk.